A CERTAIN SOUND

A CERTAIN SOUND

The Struggle for Liberation
in South Africa

CEDRIC MAYSON

ORBIS BOOKS
Maryknoll, New York 10545

The Catholic Foreign Mission Society of America (Maryknoll) recruits and trains people for overseas missionary service. Through Orbis Books Maryknoll aims to foster the international dialogue that is essential to mission. The books published, however, reflect the opinions of their authors and are not meant to represent the official position of the society.

Originally published by Epworth Press, 1 Central Buildings, Westminster, London SW1
Copyright © 1984 by Epworth Press
United States edition 1985 by Orbis Books, Maryknoll, NY 10545

Library of Congress Cataloging in Publication Data

Mayson, Cedric.
   A cerain sound.

   1. Blacks—South Africa—Politics and government.
2. Blacks—South Africa—Social conditions.   3. South
Africa—Race relations.   4. Race relations—Religious
aspects—Christianity.   5. Nationalism—South Africa.
I. Title.
DT763.6.M39   1985   305.8'968   85-13678
ISBN 0-88344-210-8 (pbk.)

To
Paul Langa 25 years
Barbara Hogan 10 years
Rob Adam 10 years
Norman Manyopote killed

If the trumpet gives an uncertain sound
who will be ready for the struggle?

I Corinthians 14.8

Contents

Acknowledgments

To the United Church of Canada, Toronto; the
Church of Sweden Mission, Uppsala; Nederlandse
Hervormde Kerk, Utrecht; Gereformeerde Kerken
in Nederland, Leusen; Evangelisches Missions-
werk, Hamburg; the Methodist Church, London;
and the Christian Institute Fund, London, for
their support.

To Theo Kotze, the Alliance of Radical Methodists, and the staff of Bow Mission, for their
encouragement.

To Brian Brown, Horst Kleinschmidt and
Pauline Webb, for helpful comments.

To Professor Jürgen Moltmann for ideas in
Chapter 2, and Dr Ulrich Duchrow for ideas in
Chapter 8.

To the Methodist Newspaper *Dimension* for
quotations in Chapters 3 and 8; and to Darton,
Longman & Todd for permission to quote from
the Jerusalem Bible in the scriptural passages.

And most of all, to the Comrades who asked me
to do it, and Penelope Thandi Mayson who shared
in the task.

Stepney,   CEDRIC MAYSON
London

I

Out of the Frying Pan

His candle in its iron holder, with the shade to shield his venerable eyes from the flame, still stands on the table before the window as it did three decades ago – or twenty, if it comes to that. The same kneeler. The same ancient chair with such a broad seat for such a little man; the tiny wrought iron fireplace in the corner of this tiny panelled room, scarcely larger than a cupboard. Behind me is the door to the bedroom in which John Wesley died, and this is the room in which he said his prayers.

I came here to Wesley's house in London thirty years ago on the eve of sailing to become a Methodist minister in South Africa, and it seemed fitting to come here again to start to write this book. Whatever life I thought I was going to live then, I now look back on.

There is still a clarity about those decisive days. I can hear the voice of Dr Sangster, minister of Westminster Central Hall, in that climactic conversation as I stumbled along behind him at top speed on the muddy path above Beachy Head. 'Would you go anywhere in the world if you thought God wanted you to go?' 'Would you go to South Africa?' It was the first I had heard of the place since geography lessons. And later, after we had exchanged our first letters: 'One day, the Lord will take your pen in fee as well.'

So I went as an aspirant minister, and I return as a criminal on the run from a charge of High Treason. All the traditional beliefs and attitudes of a very respectable middle-class Christianity were jumbled into my head, and my faith today, whilst much stronger, is totally different. Because it has been an age of funk and fudge, hiding behind sentiment and shame, all the things

I believed in when I last stood in this little room have been crunched through the brutal mill wheels of living and few have emerged unscathed. Has anything? The kaleidoscope whirls.

When Sputnik sped across the Drakensberg in those southern skies and the astronaut reported no signs of God I was not shocked. I was looking all over myself. *Letters and Papers from Prison* fell into my hands in that Durban bookshop as if Dietrich Bonhoeffer was writing direct to me, but the theologians who followed him went on up into clouds from which no voice came for it seemed that God was dead up there.

Theology has changed more in the thirty years since I last stood here, than it did in the two hundred years since Wesley died – and I have changed with it.

Leaving home to go there, South Africa became my home, and so I return to Britain as an exile aching in every part of my being to be back where I belong under the African Sun Mother who gave me rebirth and made me her child.

Those rocky peaks, the snow and cold and cleansing air of mountains big as countries with light and colour playing round them, and white huts winking to the east. The ground strolls gently down to the Atlantic a thousand miles to the west, but takes terrible leaps into the nearby Indian Ocean where a wild coast often rages. The surf once plucked me from a boat and twirled me into its depths like a leaf in an autumn wind before throwing me on to the beach where the sand cut strips of skin in the screaming lash of the wind. On that same beach, a few months later, with barely a whisper of breeze, the gentle moonlight watched whilst I sired a son.

I have endured drought in a countryside where every sip of water is carried on someone's head for half an hour; and run almost naked into the dust as satin black clouds leant their heavy bosoms over us and sent the first enormous bouncing bursts of rain to announce a deluge that drenched us as we danced with delight, and the cattle turned their backs as we dashed back to propriety and towels.

Flying in peace above the golden veld, a speck of an aircraft playing in canyons of clouds; flicked into the sky by an unsuspected wind that in a split second hurls the machine almost on her back and has to be fought all the way to a squint-legged, breath-taking, eye-gleaming cross-wind landing; skimming the dunes and beaches at five hundred feet for over a thousand miles of incredible beauty, chasing hippos or sharks and looking up to the flamingos; taking off before the dawn has broken, slinking from valley to valley below the ridges to keep under the SADF radar, heart in mouth as we flew over a border patrol with upraised eyes, on illegal covert flights to land my friends in freedom in other countries when their time had run out.

Our people are richly varied: Negroid, Caucasian, Asian, Mongloid, mixed in every way of being human. We are Christian, Hindu, Moslem, Buddhist, Atheist, Animist in all the ways of being religious. We are Zulu, Xhosa, Afrikaans, English, Shangaan, Portuguese, German, Sotho, Tswana, Greek, Chinese, Malay, Vendan, many many of us.

We are a country of vast riches in minerals and land and every resource, yet millions live in dire poverty suffering the personal and social diseases of denied and oppressed peoples. Acres of luxurious dwellings in white suburbs are across the hill from miles of shanty towns and matchbox squalor, and across the country from the dumping grounds of surplus people in the so-called Homelands. There are more medical doctors in Johannesburg and Cape Town than in the whole continent south of the Sahara. We claim to be a democracy in which eighty per cent of the people are denied the vote, and many opposition politicians are gaoled.

Some worship money, possessions, their origins, their leaders. Some worship Jesus, Marx, or Africa. Some go for them all.

The South African Government sincerely claims to be one of the most Christian in the world, yet these men are directly responsible for one of the most inhuman people-destroying states that exists. Like the grand Inquisitors, they believe themselves to be essential to the preservation and furtherance of the things of God on earth, and do it like devils.

For seven years I lived forty miles beyond a tarred road, and in the Transkei learnt how the heart of rural Africa beats. Its food is in its hands, its water in the springs and spruits, the clay for making bricks is *here*, the grass for thatching roofs is *there*, mud and dung for flooring everywhere. It bore its offspring by hand, built its homes by hand, drove its oxen to plough its lands

3

by hand, buried its dead by hand, with smoothly rounded mounds of earth.

'Thomas: put your finger here: Look, here are my hands.'

That dark smoke-filled hut on the mountain, stone and mud and freezing sleet, the smell of wet blankets and burning dung, poverty and frozen fear, the scrap of black baby bleeding to death on the ground whilst the old crones sat by the wall and watched through the gloom and left it to someone else to tie the torn cord. Like white liberals in their lounge suit suburbs.

I have been married twice, and loved other people too, and been much loved. Family and friends have given me so much and made much of my life their own. To hold a son's head whilst he was busy dying, and a daughter's whilst she was busy being born, and all the things that go between, are part of me.

Whole nights of sleeplessness; intense with infatuation; or riddled with anger; pent up with nervous energy for the next bout of cross examination; too happy for the luxury of exhaustion; asking why? why? why? of faith, or politics, or people, or myself. Sleeping like a baby for nine solid hours the first night of the trial because the time had come at last and I knew I would be able to cope.

The sudden unexpected stab of jealousy: who, me jealous? Days of dragging anguish through heartbreak that seems unending and unendurable; the transforming experience when love lifts out of lovelessness, and brings to every tentacle of consciousness the freedom to push back the limits of living, beyond the believeable. The richness of having nothing.

The loneliness of too much to do and too little to do it with. Too many people, too many responsibilities, too many hours and days locked in a cell with the cord left dangling from the pipe where a previous occupant hung himself. The loneliness of having no soul-mate: the treasure trove of finding and being found.

The anguish of rejection when you know you were right but you handled it wrongly. Church Synods and Conferences when you think: 'My God, if I cannot make *them* see it, who will?' Only slowly coming to realize that God seldom talks in high level conferences. Small dark meetings in the night with revolutionary kids from the townships who teach *me* how to see it.

Towns and cities; concrete and cranes; tractors and mines; gold and sweat; lions and that high-stepping high-sniffing cheetah; wet laughs in the clouds on Table Mountain; smuggling films out and books in.

Phase One: congregation booms because they like the relevant preaching, the new structures which enable them to run their own church themselves, the things they can do because they give so much more.

Phase Two: 'Lay off the race and politics thing: you are right but it could be dangerous: the people don't like having the Security Police in the congregation. The numbers are falling.

Phase Three: Exit. Can't take it. No one to talk to. No proper evaluation. Useless clot. But I believe in it!

So she said: 'What can I do to help you?' and he said: 'Get stuffed, missus: that's the wrong question.'

When will people learn that oppressors do not wear jack boots but pinstriped suits – or pearls.

'Please come and bring me home. I can't stand Boarding School. I cried under the blankets all night.'

'It's Tim. He was lying on the road and I picked the bike off the top of him. They had to take his leg off altogether.'

Dad? Yes I know its one thirty a.m. No, I'm not joking, we are locked up at John Vorster Square Police Station. No I'm not drunk. We were picked up in Soweto without a pass.

Soweto, 1976. Lindy in the township pouring what was happening through the phone in one ear, and the World Press sucking it through my head into the phone on the other ear. Everything seemed to pour through the Christian Institute office high above Jorrisen Street. Children fleeing guns and gas, students seeking help, whites offering it, everyone saying what and why and who and where and when?

The waiter on the night of 16 June: 'They are silly children, baas.'

Mashwabada, Oshadi, Laz all in jail with horrific tales of police brutality.

Flying twixt the palls of smoke above Alexandra township and Soweto to fetch Gatsha up from Zululand to join the fray; landing a four seater at Jan Smuts in the middle of the night with no protocol: twenty-four hours of meetings whilst I watched a man's ambitions destroy his credibility, and write himself out of his country's struggle because he could not control it for his own ends.

The police vans, the tension, the smoke, the blood, the exultancy and excitement, the anti-anguish of the students' parents turned to protagonism by police bullets; the secret meetings; swiftly learnt instructions on how to make a petrol bomb. 'Here are the keys to my tank: Amandla!' The bodies and funerals and icy winds that blew out the flames.

The waiter a week later: 'Amandla! . . . . . . ma Baasie.'

Many years of the Beyers Naude that everyone knew in meetings, speeches, interviews that were constantly repeated. Beyers flat on the pavement as Portuguese bullets spat and splat and spanged away over his head. Buzzing Biko's home in Ginsberg Township, the long plume of dust as his car sped out to the airstrip to meet us, the sudden concern as we taxied in and Beyers said: 'Something's happened: Steve's wearing a suit.' Steve had been up since the early hours doing his medical diplomatic legal thing, because during the night in Kei Road Police Station the system had killed Mapetla Mohapi.

Arthur Benoni Cronwright. For nearly a decade this man sat at his desk in the Security Police Offices on the tenth floor of John Vorster Square in Johannesburg, fingering the men and women who bugged our phones, read our mail, watched our houses, followed our cars, plagued our families, infiltrated our meetings, issued our banning orders, detained, arrested and tried us – and, in the end, missed me. I hated that little Hitler man with his shrieking fanaticism for a couple of days in 1976, and it took me months to recover. It made me resolve never to hate anyone again: I couldn't stand it.

Detentions. Tortures. Bannings. Deaths. Courage. Countless meetings in parks, cars, hospitals, gardens, hotels, flats, back streets, garages, shops, libraries, churches, alleyways, offices – even in a car parked outside John Vorster Square where they never dreamed we would be.

You can photostat ten copies of a book in a couple of hours once you are properly organized, but it gets hot with all the windows shut to silence the sound and shield the light. Twenty

6

thousand pamphlets takes a little longer.

'That car is hot, hot, hot. It needs a new colour, new number plates, and a new engine, and you've got three days to do it.'

1960. Sharpville. ''Mfundisi, they are killing our people.'

1977. Vesta weeping in my arms as the message of Steve's death came through: 'My God, will they never stop killing us?'

1981. Spyker Van Wyk to me in John Vorster Square: 'I am not a Christian. I hate you and all your kind. I don't mind if I kill you.'

5 a.m. Cronwright and nine others at the door. Fifteen months in detention awaiting trial, months of it locked in solitary confinement for twenty-three hours out of twenty-four, most of it in the general prison for awaiting trial prisoners who were not allowed bail. Murderers and rapists, fraud artists and forgers, evangelicals and bisexuals and politicals and atheists and warders. The madness in the eyes of the man who sought to kill a warder with a waste pipe, running from his victim lying with the blood oozing from his scalp through his curly brown hair on to the black polished floor.

Twenty people shouting through the bars of the visiting room to make use of their precious fifteen minutes. Bedlam means mad house. 'Daddy, if someone has to give evidence in mitigation I want it to be me.' The crunched woman choking: 'I hate you! I hate you!' The crunched man: 'I hate myself for doing it.' Streams of people to talk and talk after I started taking prayers before morning 'Graze up' in the prison yard. My friends: the snorer, the saboteur, the murderer, the safebreaker, the agitator, and the Russian KGB major Alex Koslov, that wonderful man.

'This altercation that your wife had with Captain Struwig, would that be hearsay or were you present?' – 'Oh no, I was there.' 'Where did this take place?' – 'In 1976, M'Lord, the 1976 detention. She threw a pillow at him and she missed M'Lord, for which many people criticized her afterwards.' *COURT:* 'For missing or for throwing the pillow?' – 'For missing, M'Lord.' (Laughter).

'The Court has decided that the Statement is not admissible as evidence and I hand it back to the State.'

Bail.

Saying to Penelope: 'I have a meeting – won't be back for lunch.' Her eyes enormous and filled with tears. She knew I would not be coming back at all. After thirty years.

Dropping the tails; reaching the rendezvous; stumbling through the quietness of the night; the numbness when I realized I was lost in the dazzling dawn with my only hope to walk towards the great African Sun as she climbed into the light of her glory from which none of us could escape; the sight of the willows; the footsteps through the mud; the cold swift wetness of the river; Jesus and John the Baptizer; new life.

Much of a lifetime flashes through my mind as I stand here again where Wesley spoke to the Holy Spirit. Once, once only, I heard the mighty rushing wind of Pentecost, that night by the Little Amanzimtoti River, shouting above the noise of it to pray with my friend.

Did Wesley ever wonder about God?

Who is God? Is God at all? And the church as the people of Jesus? Oh, please! What has the carpenter of Nazareth to do with these middle class affluent self-satisfied know-it-all church-folk?

The sound of cheap guitars in the back of that old Austin; in the crowded kitchen; vastly improved instruments in the hall; then in church; the cathedral thrumming with the sound of those great twelve-string boxes. Back to organs again.

And this Holy Spirit? Spirit, I know – but what is this spooky concept of a disembodied something-or-other? Love, joy, peace – but apart from people?

'You are a bloody fucking Communist! We know you are! We have the proof! How can you do such things, the father of that lovely little girl? What must she suffer because you are a fucking ANC terrorist?'

'You get insecure outside with all the pressures and your own family treating you as dirt because you were inside, so after a bit you say to yourself: "Well – bugger it! Let me have a good time and get this stuff on HP and flog it and if they get me then I'll go back again. What's another stretch after thirteen years inside?" So you come back again.'

'I know I'm off it now, but it won't last half an hour when I get out. My chick's on it, all my friends, an' my Ma she slips me some pills when I was in Court las' week already so I'll be back on it and smashing and breaking for the money and getting back here again immejut. That's life, Ceddie, you can't start a whole new life altogether can you?'

'I have come that you may have life and have it more abundantly.'

Oh, yes? How? This druggie is for real! How the bloody hell, Jesus baby?

'But what will happen to me? I admit I killed them. There was no money. The wife and kids were always sick. They was screaming sick. I just went mad with this bar and hit and hit. I don't know why I done it. I know I must be punish. But will I see them agen? Can I say I'm sorry? Can I start agen somewhere?'

'Jesus – I know you will come again in your kingly power. Remember me.'

'This oke slick me outta me kitters, so I says who you think you taking for a moggu an I pokes him. I never smaaked about stabbing an oke before, but after the first poke you don care anymore you jus keep on poking, your mind start turning things over with things heavy in your head and you keep on poking, drunk or sober. Then I grips a taxi and make the oke drive me all the way from Durban here to the koppie behind my ole toppie's cabin and then I tell him to duck and then the floppies grip me.'

'Hey! A Christmas card from Poppie!'

'Who's Poppie?'

'My Mom's nanny, ma brazzo.'

'What a kaffir girl?'

'Yeah! I like that! It's good of her! Good old Poppie!'

'Yeah! I scheme there's some lekker kaffirs.'

'These freedoms we will fight for, side by side, throughout our lives, until we have won our Liberty.'

'Andy? Dad. 'gaan dit? Heathrow. Can you pick me up?'

This is a book about faith, not about me, but you have to know a bit about me because belief is nurtured through believers. It is not a body of preconceived religious truths which is inherited, but an experience in living to be evaluated. To 'prove the existence of the realities that at present remain unseen' (Heb. 11.1) faith is constantly reminting itself, smashing the treasured representations which arose in a previous age and remoulding them into words and images of current experience as a potter reworks unovened clay. Jesus did it, and so must we.

Christian faith has its masterpieces, but it does not rest on duplicating once-off conversions like Paul's, or midnight chats like Nicodemus knew, outfacing Popes like Luther, facing fascist stranglers like Bonhoeffer, or conquering poverty like Mother Teresa. 'This is your life' is where your faith has its being.

Faith is not a replica, but an original personal experience that arises in the actual ordinary life of ordinary people, and because a down to earth life with ordinary people has brought great change and growth to my faith, it may help to give you courage to face your own reality.

Faith begins with the courage to throw away what you cannot accept even if it leaves you starkers, and that includes many inherited concepts of God. God is not a device to plug the gaps in our knowledge, but a light to view all of it.

Religious junk is peculiar. Whether we are 'religious' or not, there is a part of the human personality which is open to spiritual, cultural, or visionary fulfilment, and most of us cannot get in there because it is jammed with antiquities. Our minds are choked with theological garbage settled with the dust of ages, and whether we believe it or not we are reluctant to throw it out, for old times sake. Some of it can be recycled for good use; some of it can be preserved in the museums of theological memories; but, spiritual or not, junk is junk. It must be thrown out and destroyed, with tears or cheers, if our inner being is to be made habitable again. Most people *cannot* believe until they have thrown away the fallacies of faith.

I can no longer talk about God as if he was a big Uncle, some place, who has told me to tell you what you ought to do.

But I can say that there are truths in this book that have made me free, as Jesus said they would. Most of the while nowadays, I feel good about what I believe. I live on it, steer my life by it, make my relationships and commitments by it, constantly learn by it. I have come out of a mess of disbelief, through the confusion of what to throw away and what to plant and grow, and the new life burgeons.

Faith comes as a gift to the worst of us, so do not try to earn it by being good enough. God does not stop talking to you because you disagree with the preacher; but he only starts talking to you when you start being honest with yourself. You're okay.

But test it. Test it in scripture and in history. Test it in yourself. Test it in the love of your friends.

These are the truths love taught me. It shone through Mashwabada's bluff honesty who was born of Africa if ever a man was; it would break up the fierceness of K's stern and savage denunciations with the startling white flash of his laughing teeth before he took breath and launched into volubleness again; it was love with which M pinned me down with his strong brown hands when I wanted to go after those black-bashing young cops, saying: 'Leave them! Leave them! You have a job to do that does not include being a stupid hero!'

Love in Robert Sobukwe's eyes: 'It is time for unity now. Give me ten minutes with Nelson and the split with PAC is over. Why do you think they left him on the Island and brought me to Kimberley?'

'I am a woman: a black woman: a woman of the soil of Africa. I love laughter and singing and noise. Love them! And I love my man. I want my man. I want my man to have me and give me a child. And I cannot have my man because my man is not here. Not ever any more because I must leave my country.'

The love in Seth Mokitimi, first black President of the Methodist Church of South Africa, wondering in lonely despair at the attitude of his white colleagues, and crying: 'But I believe in the kingdom! I believe in it! If I did not believe in it I could not go on. His love constrains me!'

'When Solomon was killed, his friends adopted me. They looked after me like ten sons. That was what politicized me.' Love is the most revolutionary political strategy in the world. Being woken by his voice as he lay dying, calling with such intensity: 'Where's Dad?' It gave me reason to live for ever because someone, just once, could love me and want me as much as that.

And other loves.

Trust the truth that touches you even if the road seems lonely. Believe the love which reaches you, even if you must wade towards it through feelings and fears and doubts. Only you can liberate you, only in you can you find the good news of God's divine jurisdiction that is the power in human life. It comes through others.

So. Now I must write a book about faith.

I went from here in Wesley's Prayer Room, all those years ago, to bid farewell to Sangster in his room at Westminster Central Hall, looking out on Westminster Abbey, 'the church across the road'. He said that it was his custom to meet regularly with a few other ministers from central London to try and keep their finger on the pulse of Christianity throughout the globe, from Chile to China. Whilst he had never been to South Africa, he knew that all the problems of the world were experienced there.

'Some of us think', he said, 'that perhaps the coming of the kingdom to the world may be heralded by its coming in that sub-continent.'

I have listened for it.

For me, the trumpet has a certain sound.

2

From Me to Us

Christianity is about a liberation movement amongst us earth-lings. It is about how the man Jesus of Nazareth, with 'an unparalleled leap of creative imagination' set out a way of understanding the great processes that operate in the life of the world, and how to be a positive and happy part of them. It is intensely worldly, and not particularly religious. In short, Christianity is quite different from the popular idea of it which is a sometimes amusing and sometimes hideous caricature of the real thing.

I was raised in the caricature period, as most of us were. The religion most of us picked up (often in cold, dark, sick churches where people forced themselves to sing cold, dark, sick hymns about the warmth and light and healing) appeared to have few points of contact with the actual world in which we lived. Life is often a handful, but Christianity was mostly a remote and aloof headful. It brought problems.

Religion seemed to be an attempt to perpetuate ideas and practices from past ages which had little or nothing to do with current affairs, except that we should be good. God did not seem to be much of a God if he had nothing to say about the realities which filled the newspapers, and controlled our daily lives. Was God living?

Religion was about preparing for what happened after you were dead, and its hymns, images, sermons, churches, theologies and attitudes all seemed preoccupied with dying. But we were very much alive – surprisingly so when you thought of the bombs and shortages which punctuated my childhood. But Jesus did not appear to be obsessed with dying except when he did – and then he came back to life again. So they said.

They said I should be converted, and give my heart to the Lord, and be born again, and I would have been glad because I was brought up a Christian. But how? They implied that although it was not essential to have a psychedelic conversion experience like Saul of Tarsus on the road to Damascus, it might help. I tried very hard, but nothing happened.

A heavy emphasis on sin in the church made me feel terribly guilty which was all right because it seemed to be a way of life for church people to feel guilty, but I did not know why. Unfortunately, I did not drink, smoke, swear, blaspheme, or fornicate, which seemed to be what they were getting at, and having not the slightest inclination to try any of them I could not even feel guilty about being proud of overcoming temptation . . . and was this what they called life abundant?

Of course, it was quite different walking in the forest under the stars, watching and listening to everything as I followed the kerb stones, exulting in music, racing my bike, smelling corn, meeting girls, daring to think. I talked to God all the while then, but not in a religious sort of way.

The God of Creation, Harvest, Christmas stories, Easter services, Eucharists, Funerals and Buildings, seemed to have little connection with Russia and America, incredibly beautiful and deathly atomic clouds, tax and telly, unemployment, apartheid or the pill. There was a spiritual apartheid, as there still is for many people. Religion and reality were kept in separate compartments and there was a great reluctance to allow them to overlap except in clearly defined spheres, the major restriction being that it was essential to keep religion out of politics, and you must not bring politics into religion. In fact, the place where I used to have my hair shorn into a straight back and sides for a bob had a large notice stencilled on the mirror for all customers to see and observe in their clipped conversation: NO RELIGION OR POLITICS.

I had more to get my teeth into when I heard about sanctification because at least you were hunting real personality experiences and not fleeting emotions . . . but it was all so terribly self-centred and *me*, whereas life itself was terribly *us*.

Studying the Bible in preparation for preachers' examinations made life even more confusing, because it soon became clear that there were vast differences between the faith in the Bible, and the Christianity in which I was being nurtured. The Bible is about this earth and the people who live on it, and religion and politics are woven together from start to finish. The characters who formed the cast of the Holy Scriptures became flesh and blood people the more I studied them, but the conflict with the acceptable ideas of religion became more acute. After the war, in the 1950s era, new translations of the scriptures appeared which were not only far more accurate than the Authorized Version ordered by King James three and a half centuries earlier, but were couched in modern English that made sense. But it threw many of the religionists into a rage because people had dared to interfere with the holy phrases which meant more to them as religious idiosyncrasies than they did as words of life. But they could not deny the text.

Beyond asserting and commending it, the Bible has little to say about heaven or life after death. The Old Testament hardly mentions it, and it is present only as a minor theme in the New. The vast concentration upon this subject in our hymn books and devotional literature and religious pictures, and in the jargon of religious language in the popular mind, does not represent an emphasis found in the scriptures. It is an aberration, an invention of religious practitioners for manipulating the credulous, not the content of the gospel.

The New Testament is also quite uninterested in laying down rules and rituals for ecclesiastical institutions, and for this reason provokes continuous controversy amongst those who try to use it for this purpose. Jesus was not concerned to establish religious rites, but a new Way of life that was not dependent upon such things.

The Bible speaks of a world we know. Parts of it are deadly boring and repetitive but that is only to be expected when some of the ancient documents have been copied and edited several times. But not most of it.

It is about liberation. It is about oppression, and wars, exiles and compulsory removal schemes. It is full of politics and passion, crime and conquest. It is about economic oppression, the dangers of affluence and poverty, of formalized religion which avoids involvement in real social issues, about violence and the will of God, misguided leadership, wisdom, justice and social morality. It clobbers those who seek to avoid the realities of life by hiding themselves in religious oddities. Above all it is a love story, where people find victory out of defeat and life out of death, and how people on earth can cope when human community is threatened, and how they can achieve new hopes and dimensions despite the pressures of power.

Families, tribes, groups of refugees, gangs of guerilla fighters, schools of students, prophets with their bands of followers, Jesus and the men and women who were his disciples, the apostles and their acolytes, the early Christians establishing ecclesia in their homes from which a faith burst that spread in all directions – this is *us*. The Bible is about human communities not religious institutions, about human endeavours and relationships and organization in the every day things of life, and its concern for spiritual inwardness is to lead groups of people into the way of living fully integrated lives.

The faith of the Bible is about *us*, and so it began to make more sense to *me*.

In the early summer of 1953, the year in which Tensing and Hillary conquered Everest and Elizabeth was crowned in Westminster Abbey, I was preparing to leave for South Africa. Something happened one day which had a major influence on my life, though it sounds little enough in the telling of it.

I went for a walk in Epping Forest and sat on a log thinking of the things of the faith. Quite suddenly and naturally there came into my mind the realization that Jesus meant what he said about the kingdom of God on earth. The context of Christianity is not heaven but earth. Worldly affairs are at the heart of the kingdom, not merely the furniture in a workshop making souls for eternity. The focus is not on me, but us. God is working to bring his kingdom on earth.

It was a quite unexpected experience of belief. Ever since, the focus of all I have done or thought has been brought back to this point, or has sprung from it.

Without this concept, I have no distinctive Christian view of the world, and the Christian life is simply an attempt to do good within the limitations of the status quo of society. With this faith there is a new world, a new understanding, a new motivation, a new power, a new hope, new life.

Life in the context of the kingdom is a new way of being, a judgment and rejection of other ways, and almost incredible Good News.

It is what Jesus meant when he said to Nicodemus: 'You must be born again to see the kingdom of God.'

We are so accustomed to performing a double-speak in our minds when we think on anything to do with God, that the simple truth often eludes us. Whatever is meant by the concept, God is not a religious thing which we can only approach by the proper channels and through the authorized people, but the centre of our being who is open to anyone at anytime just as they are. Most of us need a course of unthinking, a sort of mental enema into a period of empty agnosticism before we can find faith.

People once thought that God held the heavens in the hollow of his hand, that his fingers set the stars upon their courses. It was poetic language but it formed such a strong picture in people's minds that they found it difficult to adjust to the concept of a round world whirling round the sun at a very high rate of knots, and that the whole of the constellations in the universe were actually held in place by the unseen and previously unsuspected forces of gravity.

Most of us have little difficulty in recognizing that when we speak of God creating the world we are using religious language to describe physical events. We do not imagine anymore that a Big Man sat down in the sky and poked around with his fingers to make the world out of nothing, but are using religious technical terms to convey our belief that a caring intelligence is involved in the physical universe. Saying that God is the Creator and Sustainer of life is a religious statement which we may find impossible to convey in better words, but find helpful in focussing our intuitive feelings. Yet the images linger on and try to take over the reality.

We must be prepared for some rethinking and image-destroying on the subject of the kingdom of God.

The words do not mean a geographical place or a state either on heaven or earth, but are used in the sense of governing: God's kingly rule. In an age when monarchies have gone out of fashion the word 'jurisdiction' carries a better meaning.

There is a divine jurisdiction running through the affairs of the whole human community in politics, economics, culture, ecology, and faith. It is not confined to the 'Christian' world: like the force of gravity or the rising of yeast in flour the movement of the kingdom is a fact of all life quite independent of our knowledge of it, or of how it works. God's ruling influence runs through life.

The kingdom of God which Jesus proclaimed is not a religious kingdom. It is thoroughly political; it will cost much money and is the major earthly economic event; it is an encounter and experience of human communities amongst people with every sort of culture; it is concerned with making the earth go round amongst all; and insists that in all these pragmatic concerns human beings can only find their way by developing their spiritual nature in being loving persons.

The success or failure of human enterprise is not subject to the capriciousness of calling up God in prayer one morning and asking him to change his agenda; his influence is built in; the kingdom is the way it is; it is how the world will work; it is a fact of life.

Once Jesus has given us the key to it, we can observe this jurisdiction running through the history and interpretation within the Bible. The Bible story is full of *politics*; it is an *economic* saga of plenty and poverty from the myths of the beginning to the myths of the end; it is an account of the conflict between *cultures* and the discoveries of social harmony. It is about the *goodness of the earth* and the tilling and subduing of it, and about the belief and *spiritual power* which is the root of human being.

It is as if the fingers of God were at work amongst the affairs of his people in these five ways, and – within the limits of simile applied to events beyond its limits – these earthly human concerns are the glove upon the hand of God.

Behind the story of Exodus and the Golden Calf is revealed the failure of the type of political governance embodied in the

Pharaoh despite all its vast resources of wealth and power, and the positive political lessons to be learnt from the experience of Moses and the children of Israel. Throughout history we can see people discovering the political rules in accordance with which human society can be governed – and ignoring them, and breaking themselves upon them.

Amos, preaching the justice of God to those lounging by the bars and luxurious swimming pools of Samaria in 750 BC, was not simply being religious when he cried: 'I hate, I despise your feasts and take no delight in your solemn assemblies', or forecast horrors 'because they have rejected the Law of Yahweh and failed to keep his precepts.' He was proclaiming basic economic truths about how God's jurisdiction on earth operates. The kingdom makes demands upon the production and utilization of wealth which are fundamental to the successful organization of human society. The selfish acquisition of riches, or the central control of wealth by a small section of the community is intrinsically antihuman, unworkable, and economically self-destructive.

The experience of the early Christians in the kaleidoscope of colour, language and races of the eastern Mediterranean is an exposition of the kingdom in the sphere of culture. People have traditionally sought security by retreating into the citadel of their separateness: their sex, race, family, neighbourhood, tribe, nation, religion, colour, economic group, or language have been used as centres of living but the total failure of this policy in Bible and history is a clear record that human beings cannot succeed in such separatist ways. The community discoveries of the New Testament show people who found a unity which overcame the conflicts of race, religion, culture, class and sex, and become a model that demands our closest attention.

In the spheres of ecology and faith we are dealing with the basic material and spiritual requirements of humankind. The essential nature of the earth is good, and of humans is love, and both will only work if they are dealt with on such terms. The earth is a place in which good can triumph over evil, and earthlings can find their fulfilment in love, and all else is failure.

The fact that some things work in human society and others will not is a non-religious way of discussing the judgment of

God. As surely as human bodies will not work unless given proper facilities for food, rest and fresh air, so human society will not work unless given proper facilities for the divine jurisdiction to operate.

The world will only work the right way: if you try it the wrong way it will not work. The kingdom is the right way. We have persistently tried to work it the wrong way, and have to liberate ourselves from the oppression of these wrong systems, into an openness to the kingdom.

Humanity is so made that totalitarianism is taboo; affluence and poverty are suicidal; cultural protectionism kills it; and if you treat the earth as a place for plunder, or earthlings as slaves or gods or tools or machines, you will not get away with it be you Pharaoh, Pope or P. W. Botha. Such procedures are out of harmony with the principles by which human society may operate successfully within the divine jurisdiction, and will be smashed to pieces by it.

To proclaim this is to preach the Law of God which has been the first duty of prophets, and it can be done today with all the thundering assurance that ever attended the truth, and in every detailed application to the society in which we live at this time.

But what of the positive side? Jesus constantly speaks of the kingdom as Good News, as a gospel to be proclaimed not only in warning and judgment upon wrong ways, but as the promise and hope of new things on earth. With the Bible as our interpreter, the experience of two thousand years to learn from, and the thrusting insistence of our own age demanding an answer, can we spell out the positive direction of the divine jurisdiction in human affairs today? And can we do it in simple non-religious language so that people know what we are talking about? What are we actually asking for?

The kingdom is not a preordained plan designed at the top for us to put into practice, not a modern set of Ten Commandments, or a constitution with a list of rules. It is a movement being worked into and out of the processes of living from the bottom up, not the top down, a recognition of the experience of liberation operating amongst people, something happening to us where we are.

In modern language, the kingdom appears to emerge . . .

        politically   – in democracy,
        economically – in socialism,
        culturally   – in community,
        ecologically – in wholeness,
        spiritually   – in love.

Precisely how these concepts may be defined, analysed, detailed, planned, performed, and taken to fulfilment is a major task: but the principle and the pattern is clear enough. Here in this world of us, religion and reality come together in an integrated whole which enables us to be whole people. The kingdom is no longer a cop out for *me*, but a movement amongst *us*.

Democracy, socialism, community, wholeness and love have as their common denominator the fact that they are all performed by and with people. They arise out of being together. Totalitarianism, capitalism, isolation and separatism, pollution and oppression all depend upon laws, machines, elites, systems, tools, and a self-centred universe. When we enter the world of the kingdom we are in a sphere of human encounters, of moments in which we begin to experience new life amongst us. If you like the phraseology – God is in those us-moments.

The further effect of the insights of the kingdom is the realization that the true conflict is not between religion and reality, because both work within the restricted world-view of this present dispensation. In the view of 'reality' which has long since been imposed upon us by the system called 'Western civilization' Christianity has been subverted into a civil religion – that caricature of the real thing which we have seen before.

Political and economic factors control our theological thinking, and our religious priorities and actions. The 'principalities and powers' which rule the systems of civilizations exert strong control upon religious matters. Religious leaders and local churches may debate priorities within modern society, but seldom question the criteria upon which they are based. It is assumed that patriotism, Westernism, capitalism, and white civilization are the proper pursuits of Christianity, and that church leaders will support the state and give a religious basis for all the political and economic objectives of the system.

So to a person who has 'seen the kingdom', the real conflict is no longer between religion and reality, but between the world view of the present system, and the world view of the kingdom. In that conflict, the contemporary religious attitudes and structures are to a very large extent unreal, upon the wrong side, and find themselves in general rejection.

They are rejected by the ordinary people because the restriction to religious affairs has made the churches of little relevance to people's lives, and for this reason many of the churches in the West stand empty. People instinctively feel that there is something important and valuable in religion, but they are being fobbed off with a counterfeit in the local churches so they do not go.

More positively, there has been a movement within the ranks of Christian believers in different parts of the world towards the kingdom. This realization has burst out under such different names as liberation theology, or political theology, or contextual theology, but in every case it is the same pressure from the movement of the kingdom forcing its way to the surface. This also rejects the world view of those within the churches and religious organizations, and is frequently rejected by them.

The curious situation has arisen in many places, that the vast majority of people have left the churches because the civil religion is totally irrelevant; and those who espouse the strands of kingdom theology which are highly relevant find themselves eased out by an unsympathetic and unheeding church. How can these rejects find one another?

In the action of the kingdom in the world. True reality is that the kingdom, which is not restricted to religious activities or structures at all, is going on all the while in the spheres in which it operates through human society, and those who are seeking to respond to these initiatives find themselves in the political and economic and social activities of the world.

Jesus did not find his allies amongst the religious leaders, but amongst the ordinary folk about their daily tasks, and particularly the poor and oppressed people. As a result of that contact, his style of ministry changed totally from that which was expected of him, so much so that news of his gospel spread rapidly as people said: 'What is this new teaching? He has such authority!' It works that way for us also.

South Africa is an ideal setting for us to examine the working of these kingdom initiatives in the world, the way in which the present systems resist them, how Christians seeking to find and follow the kingdom find themselves working with many people in the struggle for liberation, and have constantly to revise their preconceptions and their practices, as Jesus did.

When we are converted from a faith which makes demands upon *me*, to a faith which is offering new life to *us*, it becomes very interesting because we are plugging in directly to the kingdom. But, as we say in South Africa: 'Pas op!' Be careful.

It can be very unsettling.

3

From Changing Personal Attitudes
to Changing the Structures of Society

Early one Monday morning someone telephoned to see me, but urgently. I would have gone anyway, but the fact that she was a wealthy widow with winsome ways, and a sympathetic and supportive member of the congregation probably did not deter me. Whether I expected an accolade for preaching a brilliant sermon the day before, a donation to the funds, or an invitation to dinner, I cannot remember, but what I actually received was a severe dressing down, a most impassioned personal chopping up that was no less effective for being torn from her depths with tears of deep emotion, and for being utter poppycock.

She was troubled because of my 'political' sermons. Whilst she did not want to upset me, she was afraid they might write me into the bad books of the Security Police. (So was I.) However, her real concern was that this type of sermon seemed to be almost 'un-Christian'. Surely, she remonstrated, Christianity is about our personal belief and our personal behaviour, and it is not our task as Christians to become involved in political and economic efforts to change the world. If we can only teach people to love God and to love their neighbour then everything else will come right. Once people are filled with the Spirit of Christ they will automatically put the rest of their life in order. All we have to do is to bring people to Jesus and the world will soon be a safer and better place for all of us to live in.

It is a plea which we have all heard: you cannot make a good house with bad bricks. But good bricks cannot make a good house out of a bad design either. There is a clear demarcation

24

between what can be done in the world by changing our personal attitudes, and what requires a change in the structure and organization of society, and the argument that all we have to do is to love one another is as full of holes as a fish net.

But because personal attitudes *are* very important let us examine them first.

The conviction that we should be good and loving to one another has been lauded in the litanies of all the world's religions for over 2500 years. It is not a Christian commandment, but a human belief.

'You must love your neighbour as yourself' is the Jewish version from the Old Testament book of Leviticus.

'Let a man overcome anger by love, let him overcome evil by good, let him overcome the greedy by liberality, the liar by truth' is an ancient Buddhist text.

Confucious really did say: 'What you do not want done to yourself do not do to others' half a millennium before Jesus taught: 'Always treat others as you would like them to treat you: that is the meaning of the Law and the Prophets.'

'To the good I act with goodness. To the bad I also act with goodness. To the faithful I act with faith. To the faithless I also act with faith' is a lofty precept from the Taoist scriptures which also said: 'Return love for great hatred' six centuries before Jesus told his disciples: 'Love your enemies and pray for those who persecute you.'

On the Westminster Central Hall in London is fixed a large bronze plaque which commemorates the first meeting of the General Assembly of the United Nations Organization within those walls in 1946. With the rubble of pulverized cities strewn across Europe and the radioactive clouds still drifting in the upper atmosphere from the destruction at Hiroshima and Nagasaki, and millions dead from every continent on the globe, over one hundred and fifty nations came together with all their different nationalities, races, political and economic systems, religions and theologies, and found a common ground between them. Their concern for peace and well-being between all peoples on earth arose from the basic concepts and religions of humanity. Just as we all rejoice in the warmth and light of

Mother Sun so do we all recognize a common yearning to live in peace amongst people of good will. We do not like conflict: we do like to have friendly relations with one another. We hunger for harmony. But that has not produced a harmonious world.

Some of us have discovered the benefits of harmonious attitudes the hard way, by fighting through hatred. There is nothing more destructive to your own peace and happiness than an outbreak of bitterness against someone else inside your own head, where the experience of hatred, divisiveness, abhoring someone, or jealousy can be more lacerating to us than to the neighbour we do not love. Crushing a crown of thorns on someone else's head means you tear your own palms to pieces.

During my first detention by the South African Security Police in 1976 I was frequently interrogated by a particularly offensive captain who not only ranted and raved like Hitler, but by one of those extraordinary freaks of circumstance actually looked like him. When he had already told me that the detention was over and I was to be sent home, he decided to give me a pep talk about my Christian beliefs and duty to support the State in its battle against Modernism, Russia and Terrorism. He told me that he was a born again Christian and that I should be too. Foolishly, I sought to respond and knocked his arguments flat inside two minutes, but he wasn't interested in argument of course. In a flash he transformed himself into a raging fury of denunciation that was devoid of sense or reason but full of decibels. Years later I met a black comrade who had been detained at the same time and told me that the whole tenth floor stopped work and the staff came along the corridor to listen to the tirade. When it was over, to punish me for being so obstinate, the captain decided that my statement must be copied out in longhand by a policeman who could barely speak English. It took three days.

Throughout those days (and the endless nights) I sat and fumed and hated and consumed myself with malevolence and loathing for this obnoxious excrescence of a captain, whilst the painstaking stupid copyist took his time over every word, and my frustration built up into an explosive loveless detestation. By the time they let me go I was so consumed by this antagonism that it took me weeks to recover. It also made me determine never to fall into that abyss again – and in fact, in the later and longer detention from 1981 to 1983 it did not drag me down.

Even in self-defence then, those of us who like to live happily with ourselves find it beneficial to live at ease with others. We do not like conflict whether it is caused by an inner irascibility we wish we could exorcise, or by ranging ourselves against evil for good. We would rather be at peace. But it doesn't change the world. Cronwright has not been converted, and even if he is, the System will put someone else in his place.

Just as the practice of unloving can be a diabolical experience to live through, so the practice of loving can be a transformating accomplishment in the most diabolical circumstances.

Experiences of degradation and poverty-stricken squalor are common in South Africa, horrifying us with their hostility and bitterness and selfishness, or with that decrepit docility of despair when all seems lost. It is an everyday experience for millions in the Dumping Grounds or the Ghetto townships, the jails or the mines, yet many tales could be recounted of loving people who have triumphed over their circumstances with a positive outpouring of their personality. Love has burst through the situation like the green grass shooting through the cracks in the dirty concrete paving of a prison yard, producing life and growth in the midst of a desolate expanse where anything green or alive is never seen. Love can transform situations.

My own strongest awareness of this conquering power of loving was with one of my sons who contracted Hodgkins Disease when he was twelve and died of it at seventeen.

It was an incurable disease of the lymph glands. When he died his lungs had collapsed, a hand was paralysed, shingles smothered him, his body was wasted and discoloured by years of treatments, and his veins thrombosed from the punctures of countless drips and injections. Yet there was hardly a murmur of complaint and even his comments were shot through with his dry delicious humour.

I sent him a note once, with some chocolate, and still treasure his reply, scrawled painfully over a foolscap page:

'Dear Paw, I can't write 'cause my hands sore. Thanks for the chocolate. I'm feeling ok but Uncle Pete said I must stay in bed tomorrow. I don't need anything except the tape recorder and a ride on my bike and a new right hand and a telephone and some orange juice and I'VE RUN OUT OF CHOCO-LATE. Yore kid Jeremy. Ps. I'm ok for reading.'

Over the years he spent increasing weeks in hospital and walking through it was a slow business – everyone knew him and wanted to stop and chat and share his quiet gaiety. 'It must be terrible to be sick', he once said. 'I'm glad I'm not really sick.' But even when he knew how ill he was he faced the fact with incredible courage and conquered death long before he experienced it.

'Why shouldn't it be me? What makes me so wonderful?'

Not everyone dared to realize that his special quality was love – the vibrant vital interested love of God that Jesus revealed. He was such an ordinary boy living such an ordinary life in such a full, complete extraordinary way. He did not preach, but he experienced and exhibited that abundant life which Jesus called Good News. He lived all the life he had to the fullest that he could, and grasped it with both hands day by day.

I can see his hands. Pink and chubby as a baby, kneading his mother's breast; dirty and inquisitive as a child; strong on the reins of a horse twice as tall as he; busy with thorns in a puppy's toe or bones in a dog's teeth; working with hammer and saw; painting a bedroom wall in riotous colours and shapes; probing into an amplifier with a soldering iron. Bread and wine in his palm. A hand paralysed by shingles learning to write again; making a boat; grasping a rope on a yacht in the teeth of a gale. (He often used his own teeth to help haul after the paralysis.) Indomitable hands in a hospital bed; knitting a hat; painting in oils; glueing mosaic; tossing pills. Suffering hands, stilled by the strength of a brother's caress. His hand in mine. And most of all – the thin wasted ugly claw on the counterpane clasping the fresh young hand of a girl, both of them at peace.

We knew God's presence not as vague theory, a heavenly observer, or a spirit hovering around the bed, but experienced within us. It was a time for living and loving and being, not explaining, and we were upheld by a peace far more profound than our understanding of it.

From Changing Personal Attitudes to Changing the Structures of Society

During those days when the nursing staff were saying 'Why won't he die? Why does he hang on?' when there was panic, fear and heartbreak all round, some of us were exalted and transformed by the conviction that God was coping in the situation.

Someone was dying in Christ and we were living in Christ and it was all true. Jeremy was busy dying, not next year, not one day, but now, now, now, and the God we knew in Jesus was right there in us, and this was abundant life and it was eternal.

John wrote: 'God himself dwells in us if we love one another; his love is brought to perfection within us.' This was happening, and it was happening in me. There was a quiet competence about everything, a simplicity in constantly considering people, and making decisions.

The visitors had destroyed Jean; best for her to take the little ones and the old ones under her wing. Please bring me clean clothes; plenty of time for a bath. 'Where's Dad?' 'He's here and he's stopping here.' 'What day is it?' 'Monday.' 'Gee whiz I thought it was Tuesday.' Tim and Andy spelling one another to hold his hand and wipe his lips through the nights. Tuesday would be forever.

Sometimes, drifting in and out of consciousness, it seemed he was just coming back to make sure we were all right. Peace, jokes, love, strength, serenity.

God was not blessing us benignly from afar: he was there. Sometimes in savage anger; sometimes in compassion and courage; revealing depths of life in all of us where every superfluity was erased and we all met together; in laughter, a handclasp, a cry; in looks of despair chased away by smiles of love; above all he was there in Jeremy himself.

God was incarnate in the crucifixion as well as at Bethlehem, and he was alive in Jeremy's dying too. The actual experience of dying was given to us and it was the most natural thing in the world.

When the last quiet breath was given back into the world, the quality of real living that we had known with him stayed with us.

It was there as the doctor listened to the last heart beats; it

29

was there telling the children in the hospital garden with the lights and sounds of Jo'burg night all around; it was there as my friend said; 'I feel angry, furiously angry'; it was there going round the quietened ward to cheer the folk who were so upset, the sisters, the nurses, the doctor who had battled so bravely; it was there through all the arrangements and the funeral; gloriously there in the Easter services later that week; there in precious personal moments for which there are no words. Our feet had been placed on the foundations of living and whenever we have called on abundant life it has been there ever since.

Was the experience just an emotional block, to make the tragedy more bearable, a cushion of sentiment to ease the blow of incurable disease?

No: we knew that too. We knew it in the immoderate laughter imagining his comments on the traffic jammed by his funeral procession, and the mad exuberant party that erupted in the manse later that night. We have known the torture of tears that fall and those that will not, the desperate heart ache, the utter loneliness.

It does not shield us from emotional outbreak but rescues us in it. Abundant life is not an escape from living, but the ability to find peace and promise in the heart of it. In any experience, however wearing, you can kick away the trash and froth and get your feet on the foundations of God underneath if you will seek love.

Was this experience an attempt to avoid the problems of death, to dodge doubt? It has not proved so. I cannot gag reason, and the questions are still there: Why does God allow it? What for? I saw him go: where did he go to? Does God exist? Is there anything there at all?

We must probe for the truth even if many of these questions seem to fall into the category of which Jesus said: 'It is not for you to know now.' Yet let me share some thoughts I had when he died that have stood the test of other deaths and funerals, and much living since.

I do not think of Jeremy being 'in heaven' in the sense of a place, or imagine him 'waiting for me'. Intellectually I reject many hymns that speak of death (and so many do). Such eschatological musings are too mythological for me, and limited in value like all myths from the Garden of Eden to the City of Gold. The reality they attempt to elucidate so often eludes them.

The reality in Jeremy's dying was of a living experience of Jesus' God and mine in all people. It was a known wonder of faith, hope and love, the eternal qualities: what we have to die with, and live on.

Wherever anything in life can yield to faith and hope, and love, where peace or joy or empathy are to be sought and found, where doubts afford any opportunity to talk or walk or work with anyone into the deeps of life, it is a step into the fullness to which Jeremy led us. There, there, there, God is to be found at work living the Good News in people's lives.

My mind may ponder a million mysteries but the secret of abundant life is not a speculation upon it, but the experience of it. It is as God comes into his own that I stand in the ante-chamber of eternal life, and this to me is the nearest to heaven (and Jeremy) until I am old enough to go too.

Real living is what the gospel is about, the experience of human life lived to the full and finding divine life at its heart, shattering all barriers of class and race and nation, piercing all understandings and misunderstandings, and making real the kingship of God which Jesus proclaimed was at hand. It is.

A friend who was there said later 'I have had so many doubts about religion, so many disappointments with the church, but whenever I am tempted to run away into disbelief Jeremy brings me back. It is real.'

Conquering death begins by facing it as a definite event in the midst of life and a person who pretends it cannot happen cannot know its fullness.

Death is a proper part of this life, at some stage, and our modern attempt to replace the reality of dying by the sentimentality of 'passing away' makes it impossible for a person to experience the resurrection joy. If we face death now, it is possible for faith to spring out of doubt, and for love to drive out fear.

Just before Jeremy died he was visited in hospital by some high pressure religious salesmen who advised a course of study in John's Gospel. He thanked them, but said he knew all he needed to know already: 'In my Father's house are many rooms . . . I go to prepare a place for you.'

When he went to claim his room those of us who went with him to the door knew the heartbreak, but it was transforming wonder because God was there in us.

The Good News of Jesus is that this is true of all life, all the time, for those who seek the way of faith and hope and love.

But he still died. Love did not save him from the ravages of Hodgkins Disease: it needed changes in medical science to do that, with a vast infusion of funds and years of devoted research. Love transformed the experience – but it could not prevent it.

We all want love; life can be devilish without it, or transformed by it; but changed personal attitudes do not avert the researches of medical science, nor alter the structures of society. People still die from apartheid and it is not love-magic that will save them, but getting rid of apartheid.

Loving means changing the system which forces you to fight them, manipulate them, exploit them, starve them, discriminate against them or kill them. The organizations and systems of the South African government must be changed if a jurisdiction which accepts Christian attitudes is to emerge. It is not enough to say that we must love people: we must get into political activity and change laws which promulgate wickedness. It is not enough to have a 'personal religion' or to 'give your heart to Jesus'; the people of God must alter the rules of the land by involvement in political action, by altering the customs and conventions which control our attitudes, by planning new priorities for the way we spend our money, and redistributing the money we make. We need a new system.

The same conviction leaps from the song set in Mary's mouth as she realizes the nature of the child she is to bear and name Jesus: She says that God 'has torn down the mighty from their thrones and exalted the lowly. The hungry he has filled with good things and the rich he has sent empty away.'

Isaiah said he would 'proclaim the true faith to the nations' and continue 'until he has led the truth to victory; in his name will the nations put their hope' (Isa. 42.1, 4).

John the Baptist said that Jesus had come: 'to bring good

news to the poor, to proclaim liberty to captives and to the blind new sight, to set free the oppressed and announce that the Day has come when the Lord will save his people' (Luke 4.18).

Jesus himself called on the *nations* to care for the hungry and thirsty, the stranger and the naked, the sick and the imprisoned (Matt. 25.31) and the whole tenor of his teaching is about the coming of a kingdom.

And all these things demand not only loving people, but political and economic people, doers and thinkers in every area of society set towards new objectives and methods.

It is a grave fault of much Bible teaching that we are taught innumerable stories of individual heroes and heroines, both sinners and saints, but are seldom taught the overall picture into which these stories fit. The Bible comes over as a distorted hotchpotch, a peephole on reality in which we view the single frames but never see the film run through.

The Bible is about a world view which unfolded in the minds of believers through the long dialectical processes of history and probes on into the future. It is a book about the world, a book about God's purpose for humanity which extends to even the least of the humans, and it is only within the wide sweep of the wholeness of God's kingdom that care for each individual person finds its true perspective.

If we are to be people who live in love and seek to further the ways of love in Southern Africa, we have to change the *political* system from the fascist militarist oppression of apartheid, to democracy. South Africa has never been a democratic country, and the basic premise of the participation of everyone in the governing process is not accepted by any political party in the Republic today. To do so is tantamount to treason in South African law, yet any country that denies the franchise to eighty per cent of its people because of the difference in the pigmentation of their skin is guilty of the most blatant form of racial exploitation, from which no other country on earth can or does exonerate it. It is inexcusable and stands condemned, and must be removed from the Statute Book by political action.

Similarly, we must change our *economic* system if we are to love our neighbour as ourselves. Our society is structured so that the wealth, the land, and the power is in the hands of a small minority of people, nearly all of whom are white, and the sole purpose of this is to manipulate everything to their own advantage. It is totally opposed to the kingdom of God, cannot possibly succeed, and is an evil system which it is the duty of Christians to pull down and overcome with a good system.

We have to change the *cultural and social system* which controls our race, language, education, wealth, house, connections, customs and friends. People whose humanity is stunted by dependency, whether it is on drugs, affluence, militarism or poverty, need a new supportive community.

We have to change the *religious system* which is modelled on Western financial and political empires with their hierarchies controlled by white males who prompt you to bow down before fears, customs and traditions which have nothing to do with Jesus of Nazareth.

Those of us who seek to obey the call of the kingdom must therefore think in terms of votes and laws and money, not merely kind attitudes; and in terms of justice, not merely affection.

All my early years in the church were spent seeking structural change. The church which criticized apartheid was itself organized to keep races apart. There were black and white synods, black and white circuits, black and white schools, and black, white and coloured stipends. Apart from the annual conference, Methodist people did nothing together and when we arranged multi-racial retreats for ministers it was considered a dangerous unofficial development. The battle to have one synod, joint retreats, a black president and blacks in the higher positions of the church, as happens now, went on for many years of struggle and there is still little concept in many churches that our quest is for a fundamental change in society.

Frequently, activities seeking attitudinal change are used as red-herring issues to avoid facing up to the real political and economic changes in society that the church should be considering. Because the churches often refuse to tackle the real problems of structural change required in South African society, they deal themselves out of the game. Neither the liberating divinity of God nor oppressed human kind find such churches relevant.

The fact that Prime Minister P. W. Botha played with black boys on his father's farm when he was a youth, or that members of the Rhema church welcome blacks who come to church in their BMWs or Mercedes does not alter for one moment the necessity for fundamental structural change.

The struggle for liberation from poverty and ignorance, from bitterness and bigotry, from cruelty and oppression means we must become involved in 'turning the world upside down' (Acts 9). The task is not to run charitable programmes but to root out the cause of poverty.

Inevitably, we become involved in conflict with those committed to institutions which are part of the present political and economic structures, whether those institutions are governments, or industries, commercial concerns or churches. If their priority is to maintain their wealth, property, prestige, and position in our present oppressive society they will do their utmost to prevent any endeavours to bring change, and their method is to emphasize the necessity of improving personal attitudes.

Politicians will talk of their good relationships with the blacks at the slightest opportunity, and churches will run campaigns for developing human relationships whenever they have the opportunity, sometimes to divert attention from the real necessity of redistributing power and possessions. It is much easier to be religious than to be righteous.

People will never find harmony by talking about loving one another, until they have altered the structures that keep them apart. Women are gradually coming into the fuller realization of their human potential and enjoyment because they changed the rules to enable them to vote, to wear degrees or dungarees, sit on committees, and control money. Loving them wasn't enough.

South Africans need a taxi to love their neighbour. The Group Areas Act compels the populace to live in pigmentary purity, miles apart. Blacks can visit white homes provided they stay less than seventy-two hours, but whites cannot visit blacks without a permit. Whites are not allowed in black urban or rural areas without official permission, so they must either break the laws or change them. There can be no question of Christians accepting a man-made law that makes it impossible for them to obey one of Gods basic commandments.

Dr Sangster, who Dr Billy Graham called 'a preacher without peer in the world', was renowned for his appeal for conversion and personal holiness. No one could possibly doubt Sangster's concern for a heart filled with the love of God, yet he wrote:

> How to get God's order on the earth! – there is the problem. And it isn't only a problem of feeble will. It has to be thought out before it can be wrought out. Many Christians – many Methodists – haven't *seen* it yet. Religion, they think is individual goodness. Wrestling with social and political theories, even though it be undertaken in the Name and to the glory of God, seems hardly a spiritual occupation to them. So far from seeing that religion and politics belong at a deep level together, they dread the contact lest it contaminate the things of God. . . . . How inadequate. Good will is no substitute for social justice and no cure for incomplete or muddled thinking . . . God's will must be done in the community as well as in our private lives.
>
> (*Methodism: Her Unfinished Task, Epworth Press 1947*, p. 61)

Christianity is focussed on a kingdom, a society, and the idea that it is all a matter of individual goodness was invented by faint hearts who quailed at the task of redeeming the world, oppressors who want to keep the world in their own control, or those with a vested interest in profiting out of religious escapism – all of which Jesus attacked strongly.

Christianity is not about atomizing humanity into individuals who try harder, but about moleculing them into communities that work better. The kingdom is concerned with the structures of the community within which we enact our personal lives. We are not just disciples: we are disciples of the kingdom.

The lady who telephoned me that Monday morning thought her personal attitude to the 'kaffir girl' who worked in her kitchen and the 'garden boy' who mowed her lawns was all that mattered. Her servants had been with the family for generations and were looked after very well and were really part of the family and they all wept when her husband died as if he had been their father.

When told that they found such terms of reference insulting she was non-plussed because she didn't mean anything by it, that was what these people had always been called so how could it be insulting? The fact that a society which secures affluence for a few and condemns the majority to poverty is an inhuman society which demands the involvement of Christians in the battle to change it was quite beyond her frame of thought. Her heart was in the right place, but she needed to be born again to see the kingdom of God.

4

From Race to Class

From my early years in South Africa I was fortunate to know Seth Mokitimi who much later became the first black President of the Methodist Church of South Africa. He was a diminutive man with a most powerful voice, a saintly figure made in the mould of the princes of the pulpit, whom no one could have accused of being a radical politician. He was born in Lesotho, and loved snuff.

I went to visit him one day at Osborne Mission in the Transkei, driving over miles of gravel road, fording the streams and rivers, with their canyons of dongas in the rich red soil, passed the graveyard near the black wattles covered with stones and aloes to keep the animals away, and into the leafy oasis of the mission buildings with towering blue gum trees along the roadways.

'Never forget', said Seth, 'Our problems are really the same as in the rest of the world, the conflict of rich and poor. Because our poor are mostly black and our rich are mostly white it seems to be a problem of race, but the heart of the problem is the question of wealth and poverty.' The same judgment is made by all the major black liberation organizations: the central factor of oppression is economic and people use race as a tool of capitalist oppression and manipulation.

What then is racism? Racism is a white way of thought. Blacks suffer it but seldom instigate it. Racism is prevalent and racism is wrong but it is also a symptom not a disease. Racism is more than skin deep – the heart of exploitation is greed, and racism must be seen in its true light as a tool of greed, exploitation and oppression, if we are to root them out and destroy them. Racism is in itself evil but getting rid of racism is not enough. Racists believe that others are inherently inferior to themselves and use this as a justification for manipulating them.

At one time people were fond of misquoting Genesis to support their contention that whites were superior because, they said, God decreed that blacks were to be the hewers of wood and the drawers of water for the whites. In fact blacks are not mentioned in that story, the words were spoken by Noah and he was drunk out of his head.

Others point to the world of today and state that it is clear that the races which have advanced in civilization are white and the races which are still 'half ignorant and undeveloped' are black. But this contention requires a closer examination, which will reveal its falsity, and how whites have used racism for their economic advantage.

The superiority of white Western civilization is something in which we have all been indoctrinated from our youth up, not least by the falsification of history. The fact that the parents and teachers who deluded us were themselves sincerely deluded also does not alter the circumstance. People say: 'We cannot allow blacks to have a vote because civilization would be lost in savagery.' When we reply that the last thing we want in South Africa is Western civilization they look at us in amazement. Yet look at the facts.

If we project our minds backwards, just before Columbus, most of us visualize a well-civilized Europe, the rudiments of antiquated civilizations in the East, and nothing but savages in Africa or the Americas. Subsequent history has seen the attempt of Europeans to spread civilization throughout the world. This is the picture which has been given to both black and white children nurtured in schools run by the West. It is totally false.

Five hundred years ago there were major civilizations in America and Africa as well as the East, concentrated on metropolitan centres of culture, power and wealth. Europe was not the source of civilization, but one of the last areas to be civilized, and when the development of sailing enabled Europeans to travel to the rest of the world they found great cities with well organized societies, cultures centuries old, and vast wealth, in gold, silver, ivory and precious stones, in Asia, Africa, and America.

The ships which Vasco da Gama met in the Indian Ocean were larger than his, and as well appointed with instruments. Great trade had developed for centuries across the Indian Ocean. Men and women in central Africa paraded in silks and cottons from the East long before they had reached London and Paris, and the skills of painting, sculpture and town planning were highly developed in Africa and in the Americas long before any influence from the north had reached those shores. Anyone visiting the ancient ruins in Zimbabwe can see the Chinese pottery sherds which date the contacts back for centuries. The sense of being a child of history swept over me when I saw those fragments which the tropical climate could not destroy, from which African gourmets titillated their palates a thousand years before Livingstone 'discovered' the Falls, on china from China.

When the Europeans did arrive about 1500, they came with guns and greed (well dressed, well educated, well spoken, and with the blessing of Mother Church) and began a systematic exploitation of those other civilizations which has continued to this day, and falls into four clearly defined periods: plunder, slavery, colonialism, development.

First came a century of naked plunder, when they used their superior weaponry to denude and destroy in order to take the gold and silver and every product back to Europe. An uncalculable but high proportion of the wealth of the modern Western world was built upon the plundering ships of Portugal, Spain, Britain and Holland several centuries ago, who simply stole it. That is certainly so in South Africa where the whites possessed the land, took the cattle, and helped themselves to the minerals. The plunder ran into the slavery period when for several centuries the cream of Africa's young men and women were forcibly removed to labour in other lands, if they did not die on the way. The godless destruction of generations of blacks by Europeans in the slavery period is in the same category as the action of Hitler against the Jews. Only the money mattered, and in that merciless exploitation any hope of retaining the skills of the ancient cultures was totally destroyed.

After slavery came colonialism, and by this time the Europeans had declared that they had some special role to play apart from guns and greed, and that it was their bounden duty to colonize the world – and take the profits home. The White Americans, and the White South Africans, contested the control of White Europeans and developed their own brands of localized colonialism. This period lasted to the end of the Second World War, when colonialism began to cost more money than it made, and so the last phase of development began, in which transnationals have enwrapped the whole world in their toils and to their service. The world has been taught to be consumers instead of creators, and nothing is bought anywhere which does not trickle back a profit to join the rivers of wealth flooding into the reservoirs of the great white north.

This view of history does not deny the devotion and dedication of thousands of sincere men and women who sought to do good for their fellows, but it sets white-ism in its primary place as destroyer and brutalizer, and not civilizer.

We must not let ourselves be fooled by appearances, or wishful thinking: the history of Western civilization is abhorrent in its dealing with the world, not in its bad moments, but in its civilized best.

There is no justification for the idea that blacks are savage barbarians who are incapable of civilization. The barbarism of Europeans deliberately destroyed the culture and the economy of the rest of the world for the sake of profit, and has enforced divisions and conditions upon Africa which to this day make the development of our land into a harmonious and prosperous home an incredibly difficult task.

Do not be misled by the elite's view of themselves, whether it emanates from South Africa or Washington or London, and whether it is on television or in the newspapers or from the pulpit: the truth of human experience is that of millions of ordinary people at the grassroots, trampled underfoot. Where Jesus lived.

The whole world condemns apartheid as inhuman, cruel, unjust, immoral, callous – but what are the people like who govern this country and direct armies of soldiers and police and officials to strangle the life of millions? Are they fascist thugs wearing jack boots and carrying whips? No. They are the rich elite. They sit in the Cabinet Room in Cape Town or the Prime

Minister's office in Pretoria, or in the sumptuous surroundings of Anglo-America or Barlows, or Barclays or Volkskas, or the great church committees, and there, with their natty suitings, and polished accents they make the decisions that pillage and enslave and colonize and destroy. Their contempories in Europe and America are just the same.

Although, from time to time in South Africa, I felt my gorge rise at some particularly brutal policeman, I never forgot that they were only the claws on the destroyers' paws, a fact which upset some of them. A certain Captain Van Niekerk, an ox of a man in frame and mentality, once came to the Christian Institute to confiscate some books which had been banned, and seemed surprised when I led him to the stock room and surrendered the little pile. 'You don't seem to fight me', he said, 'handing them over as easily as this?' 'No' I replied. 'It is your bosses in Pretoria and Cape Town that are the problem not you. You are just the poor bloody cop who has to do what he is told.' He nearly hit me, but held his punch. (One of our colleagues who had heard the exchange was quaking in her shoes: she knew that we had moved boxes of these banned books to another room minutes before Van Niekerk arrived, and did not want him searching.)

Exploitation does not depend upon race. A third of the South African population is confined to the 'Homeland' regions which have been set aside under the apartheid laws to be completely uni-racial and run entirely by black people for black people. The administration is in the hands of the indigenous people through a chain of command which clinks its way through cabinets and legislative assemblies to local elected representatives, and to Chiefs to head-men and sub-head-men and through the infrastructure of homeland and tribal government to ordinary house-holders. By design and edict the whole structure is operated by people in one ethnic group but it suffers the sickest oppression of any in the country.

The ministers of Vendaland near the Zimbabwean border and the ministers of the Ciskei in the south, and in many other places, live in palatial homes guarded by barbed wire fences, dogs and sentries bought from their own impoverished people. Black security police practise torture in Sibasa and Zwelitsha and Umtata as brutally as their colleague thugs in John Vorster Square. The Inkatha organization enforces its way of life on Zulus as strongly as the Broederbond organization did on the Afrikaner. It is rightly agreed that many of the problems of black states are the result of structures imposed upon them by white ex-colonial governments but this is no excuse for the attitude of oppression and exploitation which can be prompted by people of any race. Propaganda and lies, carefully contrived rumours and carelessly discarded principles are as current in society ruled by blacks as in those ruled by whites. To blame all the evil on the whites, or all the ignorance on the blacks, is to make a mockery of the unity of the human race.

Another third of the South African black population lives on the farms, the labouring force on whom the agricultural economy depends, and the least publicized victims of the system. It is here that racism is seen at its most stark in the contrast of living standards, wealth and poverty, education and ignorance, health and sickness, paternalism and subjugation, genuine affection and callous cruelty. Child labour, often in conditions of total squalor and for a mere pittance, is an accepted feature of many South African farms, and much of the heavy physical work is done by women and old people.

Black and white people on the farms have been bred from earlier generations to accept racism as a divine condition of life and it is beyond their imagination to conceive of anything different. I used to stay with a friend of mine who owned and ran several large farms in the Eastern Cape and who was an earnest and sincere evangelical Christian. His gifts to the church always stood at the top of the list which were circulated after the wool cheques were received; he never missed a service, he supported the primary school and a clinic for black children on his lands, and was a major donor to the local black church. But he thought black races were different, inherently inferior, incapable of civilization or advancement. 'I know them: I have lived all my life with them', he would say. 'You only know your own people who have been denied every possibility of development, and you feel guilty about it' I would reply.

One day he said: 'The problem is my blacks are simply *not* the same as me. Maybe some of them are, but mine aren't.

I cannot imagine blacks being any different.' Some weeks later he called at my house when a black friend Jonathan was there. The house was full of people so Jonathan and I were in the study eating, whilst we talked. The white farmer was shown in and given a plate of food too but he hardly touched it. This black man was better dressed, better read, better spoken (in four languages) and better travelled than he was. He was shattered. Gingerly, he entered into the conversation and we talked together for hours. 'I couldn't believe it,' he said to me afterwards. 'Here was someone who was exactly the same as the Sotho boys who come to shear my sheep – and yet exactly the same as me.' It cost him much heart searching, but the next step, to realize that the difference was related to the wage structures was going to cost him money.

Another friend was a trader who moved into a small town and took over a general store whose customers, like him, were mostly white. In a few months, because he had a good sense of humour, sold good products and gave a fair deal, the business boomed as the news spread and many blacks lined up to buy from his counters. It was a great innovation in that platteland dorp when he employed black counter assistants to cater for the increased demand and business boomed even more. So I asked him: 'Do you pay the black counter assistants the same wage as the white ones?' He looked at me askance. 'Of course not,' he said. 'They're blacks, they don't need it. They haven't got such a high standard of living as the whites.' I said: 'Keith! *Why* don't they have such a high standard of living?'

Racism is used as a reason, a justification for exploitation: 'You don't understand the situation.' Racism is used as an excuse, a cover-up for exploitation: 'I don't understand what you are talking about.' But the true role of racism is as a tool of exploitation and deep at heart everyone understands that very well.

Most people will change their strictures on race if there is a profit in it and that is what has happened to the so-called racial base of apartheid, and the so-called reform policies. Changes have been made in the racial appearance of apartheid for one reason alone, that it is good for business.

Essential to the folk-lore and the psychology of South Africa is the concept of the laager. During the Great Trek when the Afrikaner farmers set off from the south and moved into the interior seeking to escape from the offensive rule of the British Empire, they had frequently to fight their way in against the blacks who were there before them. (The assertion that whites moved from the south and blacks from the north to occupy an unpopulated virgin land owes more to fantasy than fact.) These overland voyages of hundreds of miles were accomplished with the aid of long narrow wagons with their tented tops hauled by spans of fourteen oxen.

When danger threatened and darkness fell the wagons were drawn up in a great circle called a laager, and lashed together. Inside, the Boer wealth was concentrated: their chests, their guns, their provisions, their seed, their women and children, and their family Bibles in High Dutch. Outside, were the heathen hoardes of the Dark Continent, and ringing the laager were the white men with the guns. It was a temporary retreat into a protective shell from which attacks could be repulsed or launched to prepare the way for the next step onwards, or to die in the attempt.

Even in the eighteenth century the blacks who were trusted servants and whom the whites wished to protect for this reason were kept within the laager or sent out as Scouts to defend it. The laager principle has grown with the years and undergirds the whole Bantustan policy which was falsely hailed as a design 'to enable the Bantu to develop in their own way at their own pace'. The true reason was to strengthen the laager by producing a justification for oppression of those beyond the pale, and to surround the laager with a group of blacks who supported it because they depended upon it.

The government, which a generation ago removed the coloured voters from the electoral roll because they feared their competition to the white economy within the laager, has now produced a new constitution to include 'Coloureds' and Indian people because they need their skills. Those who hail this as a change, a crack in apartheid, have not analysed the true basis of apartheid which is not in colour but in cash. The 'Coloured' and Indian people are now needed to add another protective circle of defendants to stand round the central laager. The

45

masquerade of racial relaxation is used to quieten the critics, whilst the true reason is that the whites need them.

Racism is also used as a masquerade to cloak the callousness of rejecting black Africans whom the white economy does not require. The Western economy today is embarrassed by large numbers of surplus people, that is, people who are not necessary in the process of making wealth for the rich. They used to die of disease or be killed off in wars or be required by a labour intensive economy but these things have changed and there is now a major surfeit. Because those who administer the money machines, buildings and governments of the West are interested in producing a society which makes them a profit there is vast unemployment. Whatever else may be said of people in the socialist societies they do not suffer unemployment because they put people before profits and thus have different problems to solve.

But in South Africa none of this arises. The surplus people are black and 'endorsed out' into the dumping grounds in the Homeland areas on the pretext of returning them to their racial origins. Even if they have spent their whole lives in the urban areas and are the product of a marriage between a Zulu and a Xhosa or a Tswana and a Sotho, and have no connections with any homeland, the official concerned will give them a nationality and a Homeland, and having made them citizens of another country, deport them, so that they cease to be the responsibility of white South Africa. Thus racism is used as a tool of economic exploitation.

This is the clue to understanding the apparent ambiguity by which the South African authorities will permit some people to criticise them and not others. Andrew Young or the Rev. Leon Sullivan are allowed to visit South Africa even though they are black Americans who are strongly critical of apartheid, because they are promoting a version of black capitalism which is acceptable to the South African government which knows it can control and administer it. Chief Gatsha Buthelezi of Kwazulu and Chief Mangope of BophutuTswana are given much licence in their criticisms of apartheid because they accept the capitalist structure and are seeking a place in it; but boys are sent to jail for five or ten years for possessing tee-shirts or literature which suggest a link with the ANC because the ANC advocates economic and political change.

Its commitment to the capitalist structures of the West is another reason why the church has been muted in its action against apartheid, and why the government has failed to take such strong action against the South African Council of Churches, as it did against the Christian Institute. It is not without significance that it was shortly after commencing its last research programme into 'Christianity, Capitalism and Socialism in South Africa' that the government saw fit to ban the Christian Institute. Most church institutions continue to limit their vision to racial attitudes and refuse to accept that they are themselves part of the oppressive structure.

The Bible treats people's epidermal colouration with the same irrelevance it accords to the shape of their noses or the length of their hair: it is concerned with the distinction between believers and unbelievers and between good and bad but it has no interest in racism. Economic exploitation, however, is a major theme in both Old and New Testaments and Christians in quest of the kingdom in South Africa know why.

For part of the four months that I spent in solitary confinement I was in Pretoria Central Prison in Section B3, known as the Bom. The window behind its bars and wire was too dirty to see through but it had two broken panes and by standing on my bed I could look out on to the maximum security block known colloquially as 'Beverley Hills' where more people are hung every year than in the whole of the rest of the Western world put together. A scratch of sunlight angled into the room about dawn but soon slid down the wall and disappeared, unlike the rain which poured in from a broken gutter or was blown in by those Transvaal storms whenever they happened. (A year later when I was returned to the same cell for my trial in Pretoria Supreme Court neither window nor gutter had been repaired.) But if my outlook on the world was limited in one way it was enhanced in another because I had a Bible and sat down to read it for itself alone with a guarantee of uninterrupted time which surpassed that of any library in the world.

I have often thought that prisoners incarcerated in a cell with

47

nothing but a Bible must find it a tedious piece of literature unless they know what to look for, and here I had an advantage. Reading the Bible is a little like archaeology in that you must dig your way through much dry old dust and fossilized remains which are no longer relevant in terms of human value, but once you uncover the lodes of treasure you are off on a fascinating hunt. For the Bible has a great deal to say about every human experience including the collective concerns of political and economic society. In setting out the ways of God for human society the Bible constantly ennunciates the 'woes' that fall upon the nations that depart from God's ways, and the destruction which lays waste societies based upon ungodly principles.

History has repeatedly proved the Bible correct: The world will only work God's way: if you try it another way it does not work. So many of the factors which concern us in modern South Africa are dealt with specifically in the Bible.

I managed to keep a ball-point pen in my possession throughout my detention and made copious notes on the somewhat fragile toilet paper provided by the kindness of the South African government, later to be transcribed to paper which was taken from the warders office, and smuggled out. I have it before me now. I still have those lists of quotations where the Bible speaks of economic oppression, justice, the dangers of affluence and poverty, mass removals, formalized religion, the violence that forgets the ways of God, and misguided leadership.

The words of scripture were written for the ages in which they lived but reveal the ways of God to be interpreted in our own context. His demand for wisdom, justice, and social morality for all people, and his judgment on those societies who disobey him are the ongoing principles by which human beings can organize their communities. Yet the Bible is so relevant that it is simple to imagine Isaiah on the steps of Parliament in Cape Town or Amos lobbying members of the Stock Exchange, or Jesus, who once spoke from the prow of a boat in Galilee, inspiring a crowd from the top of a Putco bus in Soweto.

The Lord said 'Where is your brother Abel?' 'I don't know', Cain replied: 'Am I my brother's guardian?' 'What have you

48

done?' the Lord asked: 'Listen to the sound of your brother's blood crying out to me from the ground' (Gen. 4.9).

Is that ground only in Eden? Less than a century ago it was in the Concentration Camps established by the British in South Africa to incarcerate the Boer women and children in which tens of thousands died. Twenty years ago it was the ground before the Police Station in Sharpville outside Vereeniging. More recently the bloodied ground of Soweto and the Security Police offices in Port Elizabeth, Cape Town and John Vorster Square have housed the comment for those who have ears to hear: 'Listen to the sound of your brother's blood crying out to me from the ground.'

The parable of the Last Judgment was one of the most powerful and dramatic stories which Jesus used. Imagine a scene at the end of the age where a division is made between the blessed and the damned. The criterion used is not their race, nor what they believed, nor what they said, but what they did in providing food, drink, shelter and every sort of care not only for their friends and peers but for the very least of people. This story is well known and often quoted but the part which most people miss is that this parable is not addressed to individuals but to *nations*. It is the *nations* which neglect the poor and needy who are condemned ... It is a most political parable, a judgment on economic realities, which requires political and economic answers to ensure that the poor and oppressed are able to share in the fullness of human life and which sets out the priorities of national intent.

The threat that destruction and defeat hangs over the heads of nations who deny these priorities is also a constantly recurring feature of scripture. It is the great theme of the Exodus when the early Hebrews liberated themselves from the power of the pharaohs and set a sign and encouragement for many generations; it is the great theme of the Exile five hundred years later when they came back from captivity in Babylon to repossess and develop their land; and it is the great theme of Jesus who came to give the whole of mankind the concept of a new way of life in the kingdom of God on earth.

The Bible makes no absolutist ideological forecast of the future but gives us a focus, a faith in an Earth God whose spirit of power and purpose and love is at work in human society to make disciples who believe that God's name will be hallowed, the divine will be done and the kingdom come on earth, in South Africa, as in heaven. That faith sets out the principles by which God's world can be worked, principles which can be examined with some pragmatism and upon which not only Christians, but most Jews, Muslims, Hindus, Buddhists and men of goodwill agree and it is against these principles our country must be judged.

Our model is not that of the great Empires, whether it be the military clout of the Roman Empire, the industrial clout of the British Empire, or the financial clout of American Trans-nationalism. These have no scriptural base and in so far as they claim it they are heretical. The concept which gathers all these principles into one is a central message of Jesus, the Good News of the kingdom. His ministry began (Mark 1.15) and ended (Acts 1.3) with a proclamation that the kingly rule of God was at hand, on earth, amongst people, a movement present and active in humankind, to the acceptance of which all nations should be discipled (Matt. 4.17; Luke 17.21). The kingdom is not a political manifesto, nor an economic programme, nor the prophesy of a future divine coup d'etat, but the announcement of God's sovereign will and purpose on earth which is working unseen towards the denouement. It is good news to the poor, liberty to captives, sight to the blind, freedom for the down-trodden, and favour for the hopeless (Luke 4.18). From the beatitudes of Matthew 5.2–11 onwards it is affirmed that God is known, revealed and obeyed in concrete actions of redemption of the poor from their condition of exploitation and dehumanization.

As God became incarnate in Jesus of Nazareth (John 1.14) so the kingdom becomes incarnate in historical situations of liberation when life is humanized and conditions of good social relationships are generated in the political and economic design of society. As God was in Christ reconciling the world to himself (II Cor. 5.17) so is he present to enact that reconciliation when people respond to his rule of justice, loving and communal sharing. The spiritual and the secular are reconciled, having different functions in the same sphere, and sharing a common responsibility for one another. The struggle for liberation from political and economic oppression, the quest of freedom in a single democratic uniracial country, is a sign of God's presence amongst us ... and this is to be found by listening to and identifying with the ordinary people of the masses as Jesus did. It has nothing to do with the race into which you are born.

We perpetuate a society which cares more for television than the poverty of the Homelands; which considers debt collectors to be more important than garbage collectors; and depends not on democratic support but on guns. We cannot build our people homes and schools but we are puffed up with pride that we can manufacture our own arms; such is the anti-kingdom of oppression, violence and death which it is claimed is necessary to preserve the sanctity of the white race.

Our people know the double curses of affluence and poverty but have not sought the egalitarian shared sufficiency which is the 'daily bread' of Christian teaching. It is not the theories of dialectical materialism which are destroying us but the practice of capitalist materialism and the financial and political manipulation which perpetuates the anti-human disparity of incomes. Hundreds of thousands of our compatriots suffer from malnutrition whilst those behind the guns drive luxury motor cars. Millions – three million in the last fifteen years – have been uprooted from their homes and dumped in other areas, usually impoverished and without facilities, ousted from homes and torn from loved ones by differences in pigmentation, or broken by migrant labour in dehumanizing conditions, to provide the whites with wealth. There is no other reason for it whatsoever.

Tens of thousands of blacks are incarcerated at this moment because of restrictions which do not apply to whites at all. Yet all these people, like Jesus, 'have done nothing amiss'. This incredible punishment is inflicted upon people who are totally innocent of any criminality. We flaunt the matter of pigment before the God who 'made of one stock all the peoples of the earth' (Acts 17.26). Such is the anti-kingdom of apartheid which is perpetuated, as it only can be, by the application of constant debilitating and ruthless force. It is unnatural, unhuman, and ungodly.

51

Like magicians casting spells we perpetuate massive confidence tricks upon ourselves to conceal the fact that we are ruthless and unjust aggressors, attempting to justify our existence by hiding behind a myth called race. We know we are considered the pole-cat of the world by the democratic West, the Communist East, the Third World, and ninety per cent of our own population; we have established a society in which humanity cannot believe; but we look one another in the face and assert that we are right and the rest of the world is wrong. We savagely dehumanize people and when they resist accuse them of violence. We outlaw all methods of peaceful opposition and then call peace-makers 'terrorists'. We willingly subjugate ourselves to propoganda and taxation directed towards the destruction of an unidentified 'enemy' who in fact does not exist, our soldiers violate the sovereignty of other countries to look for him and never find him, because the enemy of law and order and prosperity is our policy of warring against our own citizens. We excuse our excesses by blaming everything on the Communists as the priests of the Inquisition cited the devil – and with as much truth. We talk of democracy in a system where less than ten per cent of the population controls the rest by force of arms. We bemoan the 'Total Onslaught' though we know perfectly that it is the reaction to the 'Total Oppression' of our people. We flaunt the claim to be part of the democratic world whilst oppression groups are banned, the media, churches and universities are ham-strung by their dependence upon the oppressors' bounty, workers are oppressed and persecuted, and four fifths of our people have no representation of any kind in government. Our practised self-deception prevents us from admitting the reality that the South African way of life is the way of suffering and death.

For these reasons many Christians believe that we are in peril not from blacks, nor from reds, but from the Lord God Almighty. We have pitched ourselves against the rules by which the world was made to work, hoisted ourselves up on our tower of Babel, and told God that for our subcontinent we have made new rules. We have prostituted our faith. The worst of all sins is our apostasy, the closing of mind which permits a deliberate revolt against God behind a hypocritical innocent expression which says: 'Who *me*, Lord?' When the writer to the Hebrews stated: 'It is a dreadful thing to fall into the hands of the living God' (Heb. 10.31) he was speaking of this experience. That dread hangs over every white South African for in their heart of hearts they know that their plea for their race to save them has no weight, and that the scales of justice will only tip in their favour when they put their earthly possessions in the balance pan.

An oppressive, affluent society such as ours whose race is irrelevant, whose laurels are liabilities, which rests on principles opposed to God's way, and frequently calls evil good and good evil, such a society will be smashed to pieces by the social, economic and political realities of history, collapse upon itself in the stink of its own corruption, as surely as the Egyptian, the Assyrian, the Greeks, the Romans, the French, the British Empire, and the Third Reich. This is the conclusion which many Christians draw from looking at the actual experience of the people of our land through the eyes of scripture. 'It is not those who *say* to me: "Lord Lord!" who will enter the kingdom of heaven, but the person who *does* the will of my father' (Matt. 7.21).

The conviction that Southern Africa society finds the present capitalist system unsuitable for its needs, and may be expected to devise its own socialist system as the chapters of political and economic history unfold, must be considered in terms of Southern African understanding. It cannot be correctly interpreted in the language of Reaganism, Thatcherism, or of Kremlinology under threat from American expansionism.

Chief Luthuli wrote: 'Somewhere ahead there beckons a civilization, a culture which will take its place in the parade of God's history besides other great human syntheses, Chinese, Egyptian, Jewish, European. It will not necessarily be all black, but it will be African.' That Southern African understanding of reality is comprehended by the Liberation Movements more than anyone else, and those of us who believe the emergence of a new society in Southern Africa is crucial in the development of the world should thus be following very closely in their footsteps.

When we come to the end of all the criticisms and argument

about the Liberation Movements it is clear that they do not see themselves as pawns in a battle between East and West, but as front runners in a third alternative which has yet to be fully developed. They do not only represent the oppressed people seeking to throw off the yoke of exploitation, but liberated people exploring a new society for themselves and the world. They have a leadership to offer which requires earnest consideration, adherence and support. And they are open to all races.

5

From Elite People
to Grassroots People

One of the most difficult things for us to grasp is that our priorities are upside down. Bigness is best. The top is the place to be. Bow down to the mighty until the unmighty bow down to you. The rich, the powerful, the politicians, top churchmen, landowners, the bosses are the people with leadership and potential and the ones to follow. Success is measured by the possession of things and the claiming of friendship with people of quality. Goliath rules, OK.

David disputed this and became a hero, Jesus refuted it and has been worshipped for two thousand years, and we must reject it if we are to discover our full humanity. The reality of living in true power and human fulfilment takes its strength from the simple things of earth, from the bottom up. If in the achievement of civilization we lose the capacity to be human, life becomes futile and only by being liberated into proper humanness can we be of any good to one another or ourselves. When civilization takes the reality out of being human it becomes destructive. Not only do we have false images of God, but we erect false images of what it is to be a human being and become something less in the process.

The comment that 'You cannot understand the incarnation until you smell the straw' is a very real appreciation of the human life which Jesus experienced – an undehumanized people-hood. Jesus' way of life was far from the flash of shining tiles, wall mirrors, rubber floors and toilet paper. Many a time he knelt and lapped water with the drips trickling through his fingers; ate food with his hands; knew the roughness of rocks and grainy wood and scratchy cloth more than the smoothness of silks and satins and plastic-coated chipboard; taught in the light of the sun or the flicker of oil lamps not in the glare of spot-lights; was more familiar with the sound of water bubbling down a stream than gushing from a tap; cranked heavily up a well shaft instead of pumped swiftly from a pipe; and fire was something to be cultured carefully from a glowing spark instead of flicking a lighter. Fish meant aching limbs hauling a net not a quick trip to the take-away; lamb meant a sharp knife, skilful dismembering, and a well-thrown fleece, the smell of cooking to whet the appetite and the lively taste of well-licked fingers reaching for the wine. Or hunger that longed to make stones into bread.

Jesus learnt from Joseph the place to dig sand for floors, where to dig mud for bricks, which trees to use for roof timbers, which for doors and which for furniture. He watched potters' fingers coax a wine jar into shape; pondered whilst women mixed yeast into flour; fiddled with the wooden spike that fishermen used for mending nets, and struggled to balance himself against the heaving thwart in the storms of Galilee, instead of watching it all on television.

We should not decry the advantages of modern civilization but we lose our capacity to enjoy humanity if we lose touch with the earth, we forget what machines are for if we make them our masters instead of our slaves, we become tools of a manipulative elite if we do not root ourselves in the soil. If you have never walked with bare feet on the surface of Mother Earth, or faced the cold wind without central heating, or lit a fire in the rain, been burnt by the sun, or pinched by the frost . . . you live an elitest existence which denies you a dimension of being human. There is a wisdom that cannot be obtained in a con-stantly sheltered affluent environment. The people of the West who think they live super-human lives are actually sub-human. Switch off the electricity and they cease to live; affluent human beings have made themselves electrical appliances which can-not work unless they are plugged in.

Tele-vision means seeing things at a distance. The pressure of life in the affluent world is to make you experience human awareness in a substitute form, producing artificial emotions on stories instead of reality, shielding people from the growth of character through real experience, to become robots responding to the prompting of politicians, manufacturers, the media, the parson, or the demand of their possessions, but losing all initiatives as the children of God.

Jesus seems to have identified himself with the people from the underside of life not the proud princes of state or religion or commerce. He did not ignore the high and mighty for we read of him meeting them for supper or discussions, but he did not accept them as his peers nor their motives as his objectives. He aligned himself with the needs and aspirations of the poor neglected outcasts, the maligned of society, those he called 'my little ones'. Jesus was a grassroot person.

He had a deep self-involving empathy with people, that type of love which reached out and into their beings so deeply that he felt as if he was living or hurting or laughing with them in his own being. Newspaper folk say that stories that make good copy are those which focus on titles or money or sex and one of the extraordinary things about the stories of Jesus is that they place no reliance on these criteria at all. Whether it has been pruned out by successive editors or not, the fact remains there is not a sniff of sex to account for the success of Jesus. Whatever the truth about his relationship with Mary of Magdala and however much we may read into it of her love for him, the gospel story itself has not the slightest suggestion of a romantic entanglement. The rich are not often mentioned as benefactors or patrons, the role which they play throughout the rest of history. Wherever we tour in the world or prowl the museums and history books, or listen to the tales of musicians or the great sages of the church or the arts or sciences, we walk with the rich, who have paid for their names to be written up in lights. In 'Herod's temple', the 'Elgin marbles', the dedication of Beethoven's sonatas, or the credit of a TV sponsor's advert, we find the mighty paying their way into fame.

But Jesus found a poor widow dropping a mite into the temple money box of more importance. His tales were of a peasant woman who had lost her wedding band, herdsmen who had lost a lamb, the unemployed and the sick, the hungry and thirsty and homeless, the blind and lame, the poor the outcast and the dispossessed. He frequently warns against riches and found the maldistribution of wealth ungodly and dehumanizing on rich and poor alike. As for titles, nearly all the leaders of society in the story of Jesus are the baddies. The priests, the scribes and pharisees, the Roman procurator, the wealthy are usually cast in the role of his enemies.

Jesus' peers were fishermen and people from the ordinary countryside and small towns of the rather remote area of Galilee. He found his inspiration in children playing in the market place, women working in the kitchens, or the men in the fields or at their nets or herding sheep, not from the wealthy and religious. He said that religious people had adopted traditions which led them away from God, and challenged the culture in which he was born, refusing to be bound by its restrictions upon race or nation or women or children or belief. He was surrounded by different political factions and had personal acquaintanceship with many of their supporters but his personal policies and understanding were so different that the leaders of most groups appear to have rejected him. He found the leading classes misleading.

For the ability to be truly human we must go and learn from the poor and outcast and suffering. We can pick up knowledge in formal education but wisdom comes from those who struggle against the odds of life, for the resources of living, like faith, grow through testing. We have a curious inversion in our way of talking about the difficulties in the world, when speaking of the black problem, or poverty, or of women's emancipation, or of teenagers. The difficulties are not caused by the poor but by the rich. It is not the women that make the barriers but the men, not the teenagers that bind life down to prevent its full enjoyment but the adults. The whites are the problem makers not the blacks, the rich and powerful cause the chaos not the poor and weak. The people with too much cause more problems for the world than the people with too little. Time and again the leading figures of the world are those that have led it into trouble and the wisdom to show the way out has emerged from the bottom.

When commentators assert that because Jesus did not seek to

promote the political parties or religious factions of his day his followers should not be involved in political activity, they are confused. Jesus thought in terms of a kingdom of God which was already present and was to be enacted in every way in human society, but he did not believe that this would be done by taking control of political parties and imposing a new jurisdiction from the top. He had no interest in taking over the Sanhedrin, or the powers of the Roman's Caesar, or of competing with Herod because he knew that real power comes from the bottom up and the movements of God's kingdom is established from the bottom up.

Instead, Jesus formed groups of disciples at the local level and sent them out to the towns and villages, and his followers in the early Christian era did the same throughout the Mediterranean region. Small groups were established in people's homes and spread from house to house and village to city and his teaching spread in this way. No central committee or council sat down to design a mission to promote Christianity in those early years, with a head-quarters building and a paid staff seeking to promote Jesus to the masses. The Council which met in Jerusalem as reported in Acts 15 was asked to set its approval on the expansion which had already occurred as a result of the work of Paul and Barnabas.

For two hundred years Christianity was spread by the voluntary enthusiasm of workers, merchants, soldiers, householders, employers, slaves, prison warders, youths and women and men. Even after the early church had established a structure and appointed its office bearers the bishops were sent to approve and confirm the work already done by ordinary people. Not until the fourth century were the power structures of the church tipped over and men built Towers of Babel to rule affairs from the top down with frequent disastrous results.

Similar patterns appear in Southern Africa. Much has been made for good and bad of the role of white missionaries, leading ministers, and significant church conferences but the bulk of the work to spread and establish Christian understanding has been done by ordinary black people, many of them illiterate, who had heard something about God and this man Jesus and took the story home and made a church. Later, they sent messengers to missionaries to come to baptize the converts.

The story of how the great Chief Khama of the Botswana sent such messengers to Robert Moffat (father-in-law of David Livingstone) is well-known, but it happened in many other places also. At Osbourne Mission in the Transkei one of the school hostels was named 'Nonika' in memory of a Xhosa princess a century before who had been evangelized by members of her family returning from the south, and who despatched a party to walk a hundred miles to find the missionaries to continue the work that had thus been begun.

On the far eastern side of the country, in the closing years of the nineteenth century, a young man called Robert Mashaba left home to work in the South African mines. He came into contact with a lively Christian group and at the end of his contract spent some time developing his understanding and faith. He then walked six hundred miles home to tell his people of his new belief and in several months a new Christian community emerged. Preaching the gospel was one thing, but organizing a growing church was quite another, and feeling he was out of his depth Robert Mashaba set off once again and *walked back* to the church he knew in South Africa and requested the astonished local minister to return with him to Mozambique where he had a church to be baptized. That was the origin of the Methodist Church in Mozambique.

In every age, in every sphere, the dynamic of God's kingdom asserts itself from the bottom up. When Jesus says this jurisdiction of God is amongst us operating in our affairs all the time, like yeast in flour, working unseen within the grain until the whole bowlful is leavened, he is asserting that the dynamics of God define the direction in which humanity can prosper, and grow on despite whatever destruction comes to them. This pattern of growth within society working its way upward until it becomes seen, being apparently smashed and destroyed by the System and then re-emerging to continue its inexorable struggle is a clear pattern in South African history.

When the Nationalist government came to power with their sweeping majority of seats in 1948 and set about establishing the apartheid regime the country seemed utterly demoralized. The word 'apartheid' appeared in the vocabulary of the world, and the infusion of the new tough line in the government made itself felt on every front. Opposition disintegrated.

But in 1952 there grew out of the oppressed people a wide national expression of rejection of that apartheid ethic. A major passive resistance campaign developed, the Defiance Campaign, in which tens of thousands of black people set out deliberately to break the apartheid rules by occupying positions set aside for 'Europeans only': railway waiting rooms, post offices, public seating, and similar facilities. In many cases they informed the police beforehand of what they intended to do and in some sent list of names, neatly typed, to inform the authorities who would be their representatives. There was spontaneous support from all over the country.

Shortly afterwards groups throughout the country came together to think positively about the South Africa they visualized. Nobody was excluded – the Nationalist Party was even included in some of the invitations. A day was appointed and despite the appalling travelling conditions of those years, when main roads still had lengthy gravel sections and the airways had hardly begun, thousands converged on Kliptown, Johannesburg, at a Congress of the People which adopted the Freedom Charter. Hastily and somewhat haphazardly stitched together from contributions from every quarter it became the basic document of South African liberation. The breath of Africa which blew the Congress and the Freedom Charter into being was not a whirlwind sweeping through a desert from afar off, but a breeze stirred into being by every tingling grassroot drawing its strength from the soil and reaching for the sky. Nelson Mandela said of this period:

> I visualized that if the Defiance Campaign reached the stage of mass defiance the government will either say to the ANC . . . we will repeal those laws, we will remove discrimination and from now on everybody in this country . . . is entitled to vote for members of Parliament. Or if the government refused to take this attitude we would expect the voters to say we cannot go on with a government like this . . . and vote it out of power.

The government's reply was to devastate. Against these

peaceful political activities they brought up a vicious battery of repressive laws, bannings, detentions without trial, savage fines and prison terms, and ever more merciless imposition of apartheid restrictions. Hundreds were killed or wounded outside Sharpville Police Station in 1960. The political movements were banned outright. The people reeled back, stunned.

We learnt that if you politely ask oppressors to liberate you, they obliterate you. An ongoing propaganda campaign has since convinced the West that the African National Congress and the Pan Africanist Congress were banned for attempting to overthrow the State by force and replace it with a Communist regime. Both assertions are false for they were passive resistance organizations and their ethic owed more to Jesus than to Marx.

With their organizations banned, their leaders jailed or driven abroad, the people seemed shattered, as if Verwoed and Vorster would rule without restraint for ever. Token opposition continued, but a cry for a liberalization of policies was a mere tremor on the surface and did nothing to release the great surging movement of the kingdom deep down underneath. Some Christians felt the tremor in the ground and sensing the quest for liberation that lies at the heart of the gospel formed the Christian Institute, but walked with slow uncertain steps.

And then it burst out again, this time among black students. A new initiative surfaced in the conferences of the South African Students' Organization (SASO) in 1968 and 1969. Black students developed a political outlook of their own which was embodied in a philosophy of Black Consciousness. Led by Steve Biko, Barney Pityana, and their colleagues, student leaders began to seek the strengths of humanity within their own people. It was a total rejection of the idea of black subservience and inherent ineptness. It was the discovery that 'black is beautiful'.

'The change of consciousness among graduates of black universities that we sought, focussed on an identification of intellectuals with the needs of the black community' said Steve Biko.

'Black consciousness is a call to the black man to shed his self-imposed psychological oppression and inferiority complex . . . to take pride in himself and his cultural heritage and rely on his own resources for his political salvation. It is an all pervasive mood touching the hearts of black people throughout the country . . . they are responding to their situation of oppression not in a defeatist way, but in a creative way, constantly looking for solutions to their problems', wrote Dr A. M. Ramphele in an unpublished lecture.

The heart of this was a profound presentation to the world of important truths about humanity in this twentieth century discovered through people part of whose humanity was to be black. It was a rejection of the mentality which accepts that evil systems, suffering, oppression, fear, and sin, are an inevitable part of life about which you can do nothing except endure. It is acceptance of yourself as a full human being, as someone who has the power to become a child of God, accepting responsibility and enjoyment in your own personal life and in your corporate beingness with those around you, and in making your own history.

The Black Consciousness Movement swept South Africa and once more the hidden dynamics leapt into prominence and sent their charge of new life into society. A new attitude of blacks to themselves, of blacks to whites, and of whites to blacks, began to permeate much of the South African society and it showed in the concerns which surfaced in the churches, the universities, the newspapers and the political world. It showed particularly on 16 June 1976 when Soweto and 135 other places throughout the country erupted. Black schoolchildren sought to demonstrate peacefully to reject a direction to learn various subjects at school through the medium of the Afrikaans language. Police reacted and admitted killing over six hundred of them. Thousands of young people fled the country. So did millions of Rands of foreign investment.

Country-wide discussions took place once more concerning the form of society that people sought and the links that were to be forged with the old traditional movements. Late one night two friends came to visit me and in a whispered conversation on the stoep of our flat overlooking Joubert Park in Johannesburg, asked me to fly out one of the leaders of the Black Consciousness Movement for discussions with leaders of the African National Congress. In the early hours of the following morning the Government struck again.

Hundreds of people were detained in a national swoop. All the Black Consciousness organizations and *The World* newspaper were banned, the Christian Institute and magazine *Pro Veritate*, on which I worked, were banned, and many leaders of the Black Consciousness Movement and Christian Institute staff were given personal banning orders. The date was 19 October 1977. In a few hours the whole of the Black Consciousness organization had been totally destroyed by government edict, its leaders removed and its official existence abolished. But not its hope.

The clampdown had proved the victory of Black Consciousness which had become a fact of life in South Africa and no longer required a separate organization to promulgate it. The people had found themselves. White liberalism had been exposed as a 'cop-out' for the craven, and liberated whites had discovered new roles in following the leadership of blacks. South Africa would never be the same again.

Most people came to a crucial organizational decision to throw the weight of the remotivated black population into a country-wide resurgence of commitment to the traditional principles of the African National Congress: a united non-racial democratic South Africa.

That was treason. It was heavily punishable and thousands were detained, jailed, banned, or died in the action to suppress support for it. But whatever the scorching winds and blistering suns could do on the surface the grass roots were pushing down into the resources below and preparing to burst out again.

It was clear that no large-scale political organization would be permitted to survive if it were a threat to the government. AZAPO was small, ineffective and divisive; Inkatha was no threat whilst it was ruled by Chief Buthelezi who could be manipulated through his personal ambitions; the main effect of such organizations was to divide black opposition so that the South African Government benefited more from them than anyone else. However, a united national support for a resurrected Congress Movement was out of the question and the people did not even try it. They trusted the grass roots.

From 1978 to 1983 there was a phenomenal growth of low-key local activity. A new students organization came into being, the

Congress of South African Students (COSAS) with a non-racial constitution designed by black students which put its greatest emphasis on the formation of local Student Representative Councils. In factories throughout the country, where the heart of apartheid beats out its economic message, the unionization of Black workers began with committed individuals meeting small groups of workers in their homes night after night in countless places throughout the Republic over a period of many months. They sought the real issues affecting the lives of local people, enabling them to see these matters in wider terms, and work out ways to tackle them.

Women's organizations flourished – fed in some places by the desire to assist one another to carry the immense burdens of the black Homeland areas and townships, and in others by the concept of Women's Liberation which had begun to sweep the globe. Students at universities, both black and white, began to reorganize. Every increase in bus rates or train fares, or in the rates charged by the local government councils brought small groups together to grow in strength, in knowledge and ability. Artists groups formed throughout the country, some concerned with literature, some with street theatre which brought the realities into focus for a few unforgettable moments, in murals painted upon street walls, in bands to which they danced and whose lyrics they learnt to sing. Opposition to removal schemes continued in all racial groups.

The churches became involved partly through the desire amongst some church members for non-racial activity which led them to develop their contacts between the different racial groups; partly by church youth groups which began to concentrate on social needs and theological awareness more than they had done for many years; and partly because people flocked to church in their thousands, when congregations were called together for political funerals or prayer meetings, to align themselves with those committed to the struggle.

Boycotts of meat, sweets, and other products produced by factories with a record of oppressive action did much throughout the country to stir the interest and focus the activity of the ordinary people on the desire for change which welled up within them.

When Prime Minister P. W. Botha released plans for his proposed new constitution in 1982, the stage was set for the next development. The Rev. Dr Allan Boesak, in a speech in Johannesburg, early in 1983, suggested that the time had come for the people to meet together to express their opinion of these new developments. Over ten thousand people representing four hundred different local groups met near Cape Town to launch the United Democratic Front (UDF) where they proclaimed their commitment to a true democracy in which all South Africans will participate in the government of our country, a single nonracial unfragmented South Africa free of Bantustans and Group Areas and all forms of oppression and exploitation. The number of organizations affiliated to the UDF grew to beyond six hundred with a supportive constituency in excess of two million people.

For thirty years the South African oppressors, supported by overseas governments and financiers, have continued to enforce their apartheid policies by violence in ways which are incredibly cruel and destructive, but they have not forced the grass roots people to accept their will. Despite the expenditure of billions of Rands and thousands of lives, and the extension of armed might into every section of the country and the surrounding nations, the ordinary people know full well that apartheid is going to be destroyed and that a new liberated Southern Africa will arise out of the rubble. But the white elite do not know it.

This difference between the false perceptions of the elite and the true perceptions of the grass roots is easily demonstrated. Two recent events burst upon the whites in the sub-continent and the world with a shock like an icy blizzard in mid-summer; the unrest in Soweto in June 1976, and the election of Robert Mugabe and his party in Zimbabwe in 1980. The elite expected neither. The Parliamentarians, financiers, the kings of industry, the diplomatic corps, the press corps, most academics, churchfolk and white trade unionists took it for granted that any juvenile excesses could be controlled by the South African Police in Soweto, and that Bishop Muzorewa was the certainty for Zimbabwe. They only listened to what they wanted to hear. The ordinary people did not let their heads disenfranchise their ears, and those who listened to them also knew the truth. In

South Africa warnings of the impending pressure burst were published by the Christian Institute, the Institute of Race Relations, and the SACC, but went unheeded. In early 1976 we found only two foreign correspondents in Johannesburg who were willing to give a sympathetic hearing to black students: the rest ignored them.

Similarly in Zimbabwe the world's press sat around the bars and clubs and conferences of Salisbury taking statements from whites and Westerners who were convinced by their own propaganda that Muzorewa would win the elections. A thousand miles away in Johannesburg, friends, who had spent weeks listening to ordinary black people in Zimbabwe, assured us that Mugabe was going to win.

Liberation arises amongst the poor and oppressed not the rich reformists, whether they be white or black. Even though they are correct in their desire for fundamental change, enlightened elitist groups will not succeed in the liberation struggle until the mass of oppressed people take the matter in hand for themselves. During the nineteenth century in Russia some enlightened academics amongst the wealthier classes were convinced of the evils of Tsarist society and so devoted to a new society that some gave their lives for it – fifty years before the revolution happened. Nothing could be achieved until the peasants and workers and soldiers laid their own hands to the task.

Britain did not lack her prophets of social change in the eighteenth and nineteenth centuries in Parliament, universities, and church gatherings who advocated a new Jerusalem amongst the dark Satanic mills. It did not happen until the pressures of social revolution began to well up from the mass of ordinary people.

South Africa has seen a constant flow of books and research projects, resolutions and sermons and addresses, from every sort of intellectual for very many years, but their effect was little compared with the march of the school children of Soweto in 1976. We misunderstand the dynamics of the kingdom completely if our quest for liberation is focussed upon changing the attitudes of the *leaders* of church or state, for they will circumvent such arguments and persist in their traditional oppres-

67

siveness. Oppressors are not liberated by moral argument or emotional appeal, but by pressure that arises from the mass of the population.

Such discussions in the so-called middle and higher circles of society should be understood as a means of preparing a new direction for people to take after the liberating pressures motivate their movement. It is necessary to make a path in people's minds, to remove the rubbish and flatten the barriers of their objections, build up the holes in their faith and in their imaginations, and maybe even beat out the road, but this will not persuade people to follow it. Hundreds of thousands of South Africans know full well that the present policies are completely wrong and that alternatives exist in the teaching of the churches and the policies of the United Democratic Front and the Freedom Charter, but this knowledge does not give them the impetus to become liberated. They remain chained to their oppressive attitudes and will do so until the liberating forces arising from below prise them loose.

Only the oppressed can have a clear concept of what liberation means because they are the ones who suffer its lack. Elitists invariably think of liberation in paternalist terms in which no actual transfer of power takes place, or only to those who have been brought to think in the same terms as the elite. Many whites who claim to be opposed to the apartheid system maintain that the blacks do not really desire the vote so long as they can have an improved standard of living, better opportunities for education, and the purchase of more sophisticated portable radios and colourful clothes. Once they had overcome the initial culture shock of seeing people with black skins sitting in churches alongside them many people would be willing to accept the innovation provided the newcomers 'knew how to behave' and 'fitted in with proper Christian ways'. It would not occur to them that the African contribution to theology, worship, and Christian service could have a liberating effect upon *them*.

This difference in the concept of liberation is well understood by such homeland leaders as Chief Buthelezi who has turned it to his own advantage whilst dealing with white people both in South Africa and in the northern parts of the world. His approach is orchestrated to produce the sounds they like to hear:

68

a criticism of the apartheid system, with alternative strategies set well within the acceptable bounds of Western capitalism and liberal paternalism. But the masses have rebuffed Chief Buthelezi and he is rejected by the black organizations except those dependent upon the apartheid regime. It is not necessary to doubt the sincerity of the desire of some white or black elitists to obtain a new regime within South Africa, but such a change will not bring liberation unless it arises out of the directions and the commitment of the ordinary people.

The correct role for people with education, training, skills, wealth, and facilities is to put themselves and their tools at the service and under the direction of the oppressed people. There is no alternative. One of the most difficult lessons to be learnt by radical members of the church or the white left is that it is only too easy for their enthusiasm to insist upon a dependency which is the very thing that they are fighting. This affects all races and runs through every area in which a committee or clique or those with convictions, skills, and resources, operates with authority over those who only have suffering, wisdom and numbers. It is a pattern which we recognize in Western society, and have refined and developed in the churches but which has no place in a liberated community. The problem of liberation is not to control bad people at the bottom, but those in positions of leadership who think they are good.

The awakened element in the elite must realize that they cannot speak for the grass roots. Only the oppressed know what it is like to be oppressed. The poor must speak from a background of poverty, blacks speak from their experience of being black, women from their experience of being women, and children from experience of being children, and no white man can speak for any of them. That realization itself was a liberating experience for me. Grassroots people are not inferior people: they are quite able to speak for themselves for they are in touch with the greater realities about life. They do not indulge in emotional phantasies about the glories of poverty which is codswallop: poverty and oppression and discrimination and ignorance and neglect are hell. It is the vision and experience which is unobscured and uncluttered by wealth, prestige and power which is essential. The time comes when you become converted, cleansed, and they invite you to stand with them and sometimes speak with them from the newly shared stand-point of liberated people.

Grassroots people have a *simplicity* which is far more to be desired than the complexity and confusion and technicality of elitism. However fascinating it may be to wrestle with some mighty theological theme or political proposal there is a profound simplicity in the Gospel stories. I have been moved to tears by the sound of the organ in St Paul's and leant my head against the cool stone columns to let the tension of our times wash out of me: but a child's song can do it. I have been fascinated by the construction of great structures or the design of human society: but we learn life-building from making homes, food, clothing, recreation and worship for ourselves on a human scale, out of the raw material of life which lies around us.

Grassroots people teach us *sharing* instead of keeping, demanding, promoting, threatening or loneliness. Under the stress of despair in a ghetto situation a depressed society may produce vicious outbreaks of theft and murder, but the normal attitude of grassroots people is one of caring, of sharing, of a community consciousness and corporate responsibility which is a part of their life from the time they can toddle. The churches which celebrate communion by fiddling around with dozens of individual glasses and the trays to put them in seem to be celebrating an individuality which has nothing to do with the central sharing communion of Christianity. The chalice that passes from hand to hand, the common cup, the shared loaf that joins us all is more scriptural and more human.

Grassroots people teach us *human-ness* instead of a life dependent upon machines and tools and measured in money. Tools are useful, from a pin or a nail file to a bulldozer and a jumbo jet, but the elite who worship money and prestige and power over things, use tools and machines to promote those ends which destroy humanity and make us merely machine operators, soul-less spiritless objects which demand our servitude instead of promoting our godliness.

One hot and dusty day in the mealie lands of a church mission Glebe I was taking my turn on the tractor when I saw that one of the stewards had arrived to see me and had tied his horse to a fence post and was leaning over the gate waiting for me to finish. I left the tractor and walked across the furrows to see him, wiping the sweat and dust from myself, and after our greetings he said to me: "'mfundisi, do you never rest between sleeping?' It was like a blow to my inner spirit because I had always prided myself on the amount of work that I had put in and here was this man warning me not to become a machine and lose my humanity.

People in the Western world are tragically undeveloped, so many of their faculties being stunted as they are spoilt, pampered and unchallenged. They are educated to be cogs in a machine run by somebody else. They are manipulated by the titillation of their basic instincts of self, sex and the herd to be subservient to direction from above. They are taught that their ambition should not be to develop themselves but to ape other people, and the crucial experience of learning how to live happily as part of a co-operative human community is excluded from their curriculum altogether. Destructive competitiveness, which benefits only the manipulative oppressors lies close to the heart of the destructive Western civilization that is instilled into our children from childhood, yet most teachers and parents have not even seen it. Some of us will only become human through learning that we are incompetent nincompoops.

We have become specialists in rearing, entertaining, transporting and burying second-hand creatures, instead of creators. We have neglected our creative abilities and become consumers of other people. How many can use a hammer and screwdriver, or enjoy the slicing of a chisel into wood? The art of cooking is to warm up the end of the supermarket's profit line. How many knit, embroider, paint, make music, write letters, or know the difference between a phone call and a conversation? When did you last drink water?

We worry about drugs, pornography, suicide, divorce, and debt but fail to recognize these are features of our affluent society, the products of elitisim. To recover our sanity and humanity we need a grassroots society.

To be with grassroots people when they bury their dead can be an uplifting experience far removed from the plastic sentiment forced upon us by too many Western morticians with tremulant organs and fake grass carpets. To share in death with grassroots people, digging the graves, making the coffins, forming the processions, standing round, filling the grave until it is nicely rounded, singing the hymns, 'washing the spades' and feasting with the friends and family and planning the future is an experience of grassroots creativity in the whole life process which runs from birth through all things. It repays a million times the convenience of giving someone money to live the most important parts of your life for you.

The church is usually elitist. It would prefer to think of itself as a grassroots body but most of its members are middle or upper class people, not the peasants and workers. Where people from the oppressed majority do attend church it is in the black areas and so it is to unprivileged African, Coloured or Indian members that the church should look for direction in the liberation struggle. Few such people serve on the decision-making bodies of the churches. Most church institutions in South Africa have little effective association with the cause of liberation and it is truer to say that their thinking is dominated by the prevailing propaganda which equates Christianity with the Western capitalist way of life. Some elitist clergymen are more concerned with the africanization of the church structures than their liberation. Many workers and students claim that few church officials establish real comradeship with people in their communities who are involved in the actual struggle for liberation as it arises from grassroots issues.

Many church people, especially ministers, are so busy with the organization, membership and structure of the church, with religious celebrations, evangelistic missions, and other responsibilities which have little commitment to the issues of life involving ordinary people, which is a major reason for the decline of the churches. People know when they need saving, and look askance at those who invent other forms of salvation which have no relevance at all to their known needs. Because the church has little to do with grassroots people it has little contact with the liberation struggle except at second hand. Those involved in that struggle go where the church will not or cannot go and there is little sharing with politically conscious blacks, trade unionists, students, or the liberation movement, yet all these are grassroots activities which arise from the heart of the people. It needs strong determined action of a co-operative nature by small ecclesia groups within the church to bring them back to earth.

Aspirants to high office in the church have to remember the reality that such leadership is not effective unless it is a focus for that which arises from the grass roots. A friend of mine, a man of great scholarship and experience was recently elected to an ecclesiastical appointment at a giddy height within his church from which he would have had authority to wield great power in a major religious order spread throughout the world. He turned it down. He implored his brethren to let him return to his job as an ordinary priest in South Africa where he felt his calling to be and where he felt the movement of the kingdom was something tangible in which he could spend his life profitably. What is more surprising is that they listened to him and let him go. Those with gifts and graces should be at the bottom more than the top.

6

From Reform to Revolution

The words of the title to this chapter are evocative words which those who enjoy philosophical filibustering will delight in diverting into nonsense, so let me spell them out immediately. Reform is a change in the existing system: revolution is a new system. The basis of reform is what is. The basis of revolution is what will be. Reforms come from the rulers: revolutions from the oppressed people. The varieties and degrees of reform are of little importance because their objective is wrong. There are also different strategies of revolution, some new some old, some peaceful some violent, some easy some difficult, and these are important to understand because the objective is right and thus the means are important for the end.

The changes required to establish a South Africa which is fit for human beings are so fundamental and far reaching that we are in the realm of revolution. To enfranchise eighty per cent of the population which has been denied the vote on the ground of their pigmentation; to replace autocracy by democracy; to move the control of wealth, power and land from a handful of white men who could easily be accommodated in a single hall to a new system that is responsive to millions; to shift the focus of a country from power-consciousness to human-consciousness and from a profit motive to a people motive; to make the provision of housing, health and education for everyone a priority; to re-examine the underlying purpose of human life and establish a society to serve it; to be totally committed to courses of action that will bring changes to pass: this is not to reform a society but to revolutionize it. South Africa has always been a reformist society in which the rulers of the day enacted laws or

74

made concessions to further the oppressive policy. The country's rulers have always been on the defensive. Because the fundamental fact of oppression has never been removed, the reformist words to attempt to provide it with a respectable Christian name have constantly fallen into disrepute, and politicians and press have vied with one another to update an alternative nomenclature.

Colour bar, white supremacy, apartheid, separate development, community development, and plural development are all different ways of pronouncing oppression and exploitation. Since Jan Van Riebeeck planted his boundary hedge in 1652 the policy of herding blacks into separate areas where they can be contained and controlled has been continued to this day. The slave quarters became locations, townships, Bantu Communities, but they were all ghettos. Kaffraria became Native Territories, Reserves, Bantustans, Homelands and Independent States but they are still dumping grounds for people who are not required.

If the early white settlers could revisit South Africa today they would be amazed at our motor cars, roadways, electricity, aircraft, and bikinis, but would notice that after three centuries of development and reform we still treat the natives as natives. To a person nurtured in the type of society which likes to think it is Christian and civilized, reform has a rather godly sound, and revolution is dark and devilish, but the reverse is often the case. Reform means improving, adapting, adjusting, refining something which is fundamentally correct, but the kingdom of God is concerned with fundamental change. The concept of a gradual development towards utopia has no place in the faith, nor in South Africa.

Gradual 'improvements' and 'relaxations' of apartheid regulations are designed specifically to prevent the total irradication of economic and political discrimination which is at its heart. Many church people aspire to be reformists, and seek ways in which they can improve the situation, but they are misguided. Can one teach a lion to be a vegetarian?

My concern at this stage is not the means of revolution, but the objective. Revolution is not necessarily violent. You can have a revolution in manners, in habits, in taste, in fashion, or in life style. Television has revolutionized many customs, promoted new industries and demoted others, opened new careers and closed others, and changed the direction and content of much thinking, sport, entertainment, political life, marketing, religious customs, and the susceptibility of the public to suggestion. It was a revolution that used much guile and greed, but did not depend on guns. Not all revolutions are gun solutions.

Reforms are cosmetic, feature fiddling exercises: revolution is surgical. Reforms may change the diet, but revolutions change the life style. For want of words: 'Christendom' is reformist, but 'Christianity' is revolution.

We have been indoctrinated to believe that reform is acceptable and revolution reprehensible. Whether it is in eighteenth-century England, nineteenth-century Russia, or twentieth-century South Africa, reform is seen as the occupation of respectable gentlemen, and revolution as an uprising of unruly elements. Reform smacks of silver and glass and double damask dinner napkins, and revolution of a hunk of bread dunked in a mug of soup. Reform comes from the top down, and thus is acceptable. Revolution comes from the bottom up and is just not the way to behave.

This judgment is a carefully contrived conceit into which we have been duly indoctrinated and from which we must be liberated, and this liberation is assisted by Jesus of Nazareth who was a thorough-going revolutionary if ever there was one.

Jesus *was* a revolutionary. There is no suggestion that he saw his role as that of a respectable liberal concerned to establish himself within the approval of the authorities and slowly change them by his example. The ruling belief of Jesus' life was his conviction of the presence of a divine jurisdiction within the affairs of this life, and he lived in harmony with that kingdom. He did not set himself up on the basis of the concepts and ideals of others, and try to improve them, but on the basis of the kingdom. This in itself directed him towards fundamental changes and brought him into almost constant conflict with those who championed the status quo.

There is some evidence that in the first flush of his enthusiasm Jesus expected everyone to throw off their heresies and follow the beliefs which were so clear to him, but this did not happen. He soon discovered the boundless ingenuity of those who sought to preserve their own priorities by religious argument if you gave them the time to work it out. His approach was frequently direct, deliberate, confrontational.

In his brief matter-of-factual account of Jesus, Mark sets out this revolutionary character of Jesus in the first few pages. Nothing of the baby Jesus appears in Mark – he plunges straight into the adult impression. Ten sentences establish Jesus as the one for whom the Old Testament theme of revolutionary prophetism was prepared. He is not in the tradition of reformist priests seeking to reinforce the Jewish religious system, but of the fearless preachers like Amos, proclaiming the destruction of evil social systems and the promise of a new dispensation for which Jesus coined the phrase: 'The good news of the kingdom of God is close at hand.'

Six centuries before, Amos, a country shepherd, had burst into the pages of history by denouncing the evil ways of the leaders of the nation. In his short book, which has come down to us, the political and religious comments overlap because, like all the prophets, Amos saw the whole of life in terms of an integrated and integrating God. In the name of God he condemns the leaders for the mockery of their religious observances, and nationalism, and a list of social political and economic activity which sounds as if it were written today: compulsory removal schemes, internecine warfare, false ancestral gods, the corruption of the courts, the destruction of justice and integrity, the exploitation of the poor and needy, and the impending doom which threatened the nation because of these iniquities.

Jesus also came with a teaching that was radical. The people said: 'Here is a teaching that is new, and with authority behind it' (Mark 1.27). Jesus did not deny the role of the religious or the priests, indeed he supported them and had religious concerns himself but in both his words and his actions he exhibited signs of new concepts of belief and behaviour. When the priests and teachers and lawyers, seeing a threat to their vested interests, sought to restrain or disprove him Jesus had no hesitation in opposing them quite openly.

His ability to cast out 'evil spirits' with a word or a touch of his presence instead of by lengthy and expensive incantations was totally unexpected. He made short work of the popular assumption that sickness or poverty was a sign of God's displeasure and cut through fears and prejudices. Because of religious and ethnic animosity stretching back six hundred years, the Jews had nothing to do with the Samaritans. Jesus deliberately befriended a Samaritan woman and cast the hero of one of his most famous stories as a Samaritan. Respectable people had clear taboos, undergirded by religious arguments, which applied a type of social apartheid or ostracism to many of the ordinary people – the 'publicans and sinners'. Jesus did not start a collection for them, or suggest that Pharisees pray for them, or run a mission for them: he befriended them.

Faced with many rules and regulations relating to religious customs to do with the Sabbath, or fasting, or washing, Jesus did not suggest a research project to evaluate their origin, relevance and value. He broke them. He told the people point blank that in permitting their religious traditions to supplant the ways of God they had left those ways – and he scandalized the authorities by ignoring those traditions, even though they conspired to kill him for his challenge.

Righteous Jews – like righteous people of all ages – sought to persuade themselves that they could justify their retention of undue profits by becoming known for philanthropies, but Jesus disputed the Jewish belief (like the Western) that God rewards the righteous with riches and told them affluence was dangerous; he outraged some notable wealthy persons by suggesting their salvation was in giving their goods away. He committed himself to spreading the concept and acceptance of the kingdom.

The respectable religious people of Jesus' time were filled with horror and revulsion against him because he challenged the very fundamentals of the society in which they lived. They thought he was mad or criminal, and he was done to death with all the violence of civil and religious authority because his impact upon their society was too good to be permitted to be true.

He was a revolutionary even if he never swung a sword to slice into human skin, or smelt the oily tang of an AK47. Jesus was never in the reform business: he was a liberator. He did not ask the Temple money changers to lower their prices. He threw them out.

What changed me from a reformer who hoped to push society into shape, into a revolutionary who sought to turn society upside down? People. It was personal knowledge of those whose need of salvation was far beyond the objectives of reform, and knowing those who were citizens of a new world and committed to bring new life.

From the beginning there was a fundamental point of difference between me and many of my peers in the church; I was concerned for God's will to be done in the world and saw the church as an instrument in his hand; many were concerned to build up the church, and hoped for a possible spin off in the world. They saw, and frequently argued, that it was necessary for the church to be involved in social issues in order to improve the image and power of the church. I saw it as a tool of salvation for people.

Tsomo Mission in the Transkei, to which I was appointed in 1959, spread over a vast area with thirty churches from the mission church which seated hundreds, to rough rondavels with thatched roofs, built by the local people from the materials they could glean from the earth about them. Three ministers went 'on circuit' through these societies and between us we could visit them once a quarter, weekly services being taken by lay preachers. A visit from a minister was a major occasion. The day would commence with a long drive over gravel roads, which could be a bone shaking dusty trek in the dry weather, or an adventure with skids and flooded rivers in the rains, or icy cold in the winter. Events began when the sun was warm enough, and usually included a meeting with the leaders, baptisms, confirmations, worship, and the communion service, interspersed with lunch.

At some centres where a number of 'wealthy' teachers or peasant farmers were involved, it was the custom for lunch to be a feast on the usual British Sunday luncheon style, with everything including a complete dining room suite and dinner service carried on people's heads to convert the local school room into a sumptuous dining room. The only thing missing was the white-gloved butler. In such a fashion it was their custom to meet and do honour to this 'umongameli' or super-intendent minister who was well dressed, well spoken, well educated, appointed from the heights of a far off Conference to be the leader of the local church, and naturally, white. Everyone spoke English.

At the poorer centres, the same service would occur, but in totally different circumstances. Perhaps women had dresses, but most wore blankets; most of the men were six hundred miles away for most of the year as migrant labourers in cities or mines, but a few aged or middle aged men were around (except at Christmas when most had leave and came home). As you came near to the church you would pass the people with waves and hoots, walking along with shoes on their heads until they put them on to be cultivated and civilized as they approached church.

The small church buildings would have two or three small openings in the walls to serve as windows – frames and glass were too expensive – and a few rough wooden benches on the clean swept mud and dung floors. Those benches, rough in the extreme, were often the pride of a man's life, who had laboured for weeks to make them with old broken hand tools gleaned in some long distant scrounge behind a store, or perhaps a leftover from his working days in a distant city.

When the time came for food there would be usually some form of meat, perhaps a chicken, and chunks of home made bread wiped in the fat, or jam. There were never enough plates or cutlery so these would be passed round as each one ate their share, and then hot tea. All the conversation would be in Xhosa, and from a stilted beginning within a few minutes a loud and enthusiastic discussion would be unleashed.

One day I noticed that beside several of these small remote churches was a dilapidated rondavel with a collapsed roof, and discovered this dated from before the days of motor cars, when ministers went everywhere on foot, or horseback and required somewhere to spend the night. This produced a torrent of reminiscence and it became evident that the ministry people valued had been from those who had come and lived with them in the old days, not the modern ones who came by car and did their priestly functions and nipped back to their cosy lounge in the mission house thirty miles away.

Although the people lived and held weekly services in their own villages on the slopes of a valley and its surrounding hills, I found they all came to one village by the road for the minister's visit because he could not get his car into remoter areas. I asked how long since they had seen a minister in their own homes and this produced a cascading argument, with much digression and reference to local historical events, which made it clear that no minister had visited these remoter areas for over thirty years. Ask a silly question. The next time I went to that area they met us with horses – where they found one strong enough for me I do not know – and a couple of painful hours later we had a service over the hill, and visited some of the sick and frail with communion, to which they attached so much concern.

Mother Mayekiso had been bedridden for years, cared for by her daughter who was also widowed and elderly, barely subsisting on a meagre diet provided from the fringes of other destitute families. She lived in a small hut of one room, smaller than a prison cell, walled with wattle branches daubed in mud, a broken wooden door, and a thatched roof so low that I could barely stand. Her possessions were laid out in a cupboard made of old wooden boxes, polished and scrubbed smooth from long use, with a fragment of threadbare curtain pinned across the front, and a rickety chair that a hundred years before had been thrown from some long forgotten dining suite and started the journey through second hand shops and trucks and the tops of buses to its final discard in this decayed hut.

For our visit, the floor had been smeared anew and smelt sweetly of that fresh dungy smell that soon disappears with dry weather and a good polish. Mrs Mayekiso lay on the old iron bed, wearing her Manyano uniform with its scarlet blouse and spreading white stiffly starched collar, and the white cloth on her head. A few local people crowded into the hut also, and on the tiny·table next to her bed we set out the elements of our simple religious rite, beside some veld flowers in a jam tin. Bread and wine are offered in gold and silver on the marble altars of vastly expensive cathedrals but it is in homes like this that you catch the atmosphere of the Upper Room though Xhosa is spoken instead of the original Aramaic, and in sharing the peace with these old gnarled hands there is a communion that unites with all that is good and full of hope for humans. This is what Jesus was about: going into some old home to realize and celebrate the fullness of life, and sharing an uplifting moment in the human spirit. This frail elderly woman, impoverished, diseased, neglected, so soon to die, is a Queen of Heaven. And bloody flies everywhere.

That is the stuff of Christian revolution: reform is not enough.

Twenty miles of tortuous telephone lines, winding down from the mountains, brought us the message of a young mother who was likely to die from a complicated child birth. It was a bad trip at the best of times, but on that day the heavens were opened and we doubted if the road would be passable. With four wheels catching what grasp they could, the Land Rover thrust off on its long journey, panting up the muddy slopes with racing engine and churning wheels, crawling round the slippery edge of rocky escarpments, butting a bow-wave through the raging brown waters of flooded streams, climbing slowly and not so surely to the place where the tops of the mountains were lost in the clutch of the clouds. And everything cold, clammy, dripping, chilled to quietness.

There were four of us on board – a guide who knew the way, an interpreter who knew the language, the doctor striving at the wheel, and myself as a passenger. The doctor had asked me to go for 'moral support' – a polite way of ensuring someone else to help push when we got stuck in the mud. In time we reached the end of the road, and set out on foot over the veld, blackened by the recent burning of the grass, pierced with fresh green shoots of another season's grass struggling out to meet the rain.

Three mud walled huts, with smoke seeping through their thatch, loomed up through the mist and a savage dog thrust at the chain that alone restrained him from tearing us to pieces. An old woman hobbled out into the rain and led us to a hut – six foot to the eaves, and fourteen feet across. The door was a rough opening, five feet high and eighteen inches wide. There were no windows – the only ventilation was provided by two biscuit tins, six inches square, which had been built into the walls. How people could live in such a choking dingy atmosphere was a marvel – and a baby had been born here. Coughing, we ducked down under the smoke. The floor of mud and dung was swept to a hearth at the centre, two feet in diameter, in which a fire was burning under a three legged pot. The interpreter threw the worst of the smoking wood outside and stepping back in the gloom to avoid the swing of his arm, I looked down by my heel and there was the baby, wrapped in half an old blanket. Beside her lay the mother, and despite the dim daylight outside, the doctor went to his examination with the light of a torch.

Against the wall crouched three old ladies, their lined faces swathed in the blanket headdress, their blankets pinned round their shoulders, their long skirts and sacking aprons wrapped round their legs. They had eyes only for the doctor and the frightened patient, who had been through so much and now lay rigid in the torch light, her skirt held out as a shield from the interpreter's eyes.

'Turn over.'

'Breathe deeply.'

'Tell her to do as I say – I'm not going to hurt her.'

'Does this hurt?'

... and so it went. A swirling flick to release the fluid, a slight crack as the phial was opened, a silver gleam as the hypodermic was filled.

'Tell them to mind these pieces of glass on the floor.'

White cotton wool dabs on black skin. The three old dears turned their faces to the wall, wincing their dark features in horror as the needle plunged home.

While injection number two was proceeding, I looked round the walls, and especially at the smoke curled under the blackened thatch and grimy branches which formed the roof. Heaven alone knows where the father was – probably a mile underground and six hundred miles away sweating out his shift in a gold mine, knowing nothing of the drama in his home kraal or of his daughter, Nontuli. Everything was stacked against her.

When our daughter was born Penelope also had rather a difficult time. It took us fifteen minutes to reach the hospital, there was no danger of infection, everything was crisp and clean and competent, light and health were everywhere: it was hard, but relaxed: okay. Our doctor and nurses wrapped us in warmth and confidence. We held hands and talked with our eyes as well as with our lips while her body muscles pressed and flexed, and when our daughter slid into life with her funny chinless face, yawning and calling, her small hands opened to a world that welcomed her with peace and joy, delight and hope. Later, lying in Penelope's arms as the morning sun flooded the Witwatersrand with a glorious golden splendour of promise that neither of us will ever forget, she had everything going for her. We called her Bongi.

Both those girl babies lived, as it happened, though the infant mortality rate for whites in Johannesburg is 10 per 1000 births, and in the Transkei it is 140. I don't know whether Nontuli survived thereafter or if she was one of the high percentage of black children who die before they are five: 95.2 per cent of blacks die before they are sixty. I only know that if the Nontulis are to have the opportunities of the Bongis we shall not do it by polite speeches and gradual adjustments or by leaving it to people's goodwill. There is one doctor to six hundred people in the urban areas of South Africa, and only one to twenty thousand in the Ciskei and Transkei. The richest country in Africa, to wallow in whose luxury the tourists flood from all over the Western world, has a large proportion of its population suffering from malnutrition, a massive rate of tuberculosis, and constant outbreaks of cholera which could be eradicated very quickly if we made fundamental changes in our socio-economic system.

Gradual reforms cannot keep pace with the yearly increase. It requires a total re-evaluation of our priorities and human responsibilities and financial structures. The solution is a revolutionary task requiring the weight of the whole nation behind it.

After many years of struggle, the Methodist Synods in the Northern Transvaal became non-racial, and blacks and whites met together to discuss the affairs of the church. The political necessity of winning black votes had underlined the theological necessity of listening to black voices, and progress was being made not only at Synod meetings but at informal meetings in the circuits and homes from time to time. A new spirit came into the meetings of Synod over those years, and friendships developed at tea breaks and meal times as well as the formal sessions.

And then an incredibly thick-headed white minister arrived at Synod wearing the uniform of a chaplain in the South African Defence Force. It is not a uniform you can miss; the khaki cloth is somewhat of a contrast to the dark suiting favoured at parsonical functions, and literally to crown it, the chaplain's cap has a purple cover, as if dreams of wearing a bishops stock have gone to his head.

The buzz of the pre-Synod talk in the foyer died away abruptly as this well-pressed apparition strolled into the gathering a little self-conscious of his sartorial elegance maybe, but quite unaware that he was producing the effect of a bombshell without needing an explosion. No one would deny that people require spiritual solace whatever their occupation, and the ministry to soldiers has not been seriously questioned. But to dress the gospel in an army uniform is quite different. Those of us who have had long discussions with ministers who have gone into the SADF know how totally indoctrinated they become in the propoganda of their masters . . . but for black ministers it needed no argument. The mere sight of a minister in the uniform of the oppressor's army was enough to banish all thoughts of reform, and reinforce their commitment to total change; and an immediate change of clothing there and then before Synod could continue.

Contrasts. Lunch at the Rand Club in Johannesburg, haunt of the wealthy and high and mighty, the pillars of finance, the diplomats, the press barons, everyone who was anyone, the people who are where it is at, old boy. Years of practice have given to such institutions an aplomb, a comfortable assurance that shields and surrounds them from all harm like the everlasting arms, and there is something aesthetically satisfying about the surroundings and gastronomically satisfying about the menu. And we are very clever and influential, and committed to good works, and the Christian culture we have inherited and are responsible for passing on will undoubtedly prevail against the uncouth and the 'commies'. Chandeliers sparkling in the silver at lunchtime.

A few nights later, arriving unannounced at Ginsberg location outside Kingwilliamstown, at the home of Steve Biko. I had not met either his mother or his wife before, and a friend came to identify me, before a youth took me on a dark and stumbling walk between the houses to a small room where half a dozen men sat on the floor in a room, with Steve in that extraordinary ex-army-surplus overcoat that covered his long frame and kept him warm but looked so utterly incongruous. Several of those men were banned and merely to be there was a crime. Two were to be killed by the regime. One flickering candle. A whip round to raise enough money for Thenjiwe to disappear into the night to find an after hours bottle of scotch to greet my arrival. Much serious discussion and learning and laughter. Moving stiff limbs because it is cold and crushing sitting on the floor.

It is these in the candle-lit poverty bent on total change whose lives are open to the kingdom of God, and those discussing kindly reforms under the chandeliers who are the barriers to it.

Reform is not an option in South Africa. Apartheid cannot be reformed or improved, or changed: it must be scrapped. It cannot be domesticated for human use: it is a people eater by nature. It cannot be cured with careful treatment: it is a cancerous growth that must be cut out and put into the oven and incinerated out of existence. It is not something to be forgiven and redeemed, but something to be destroyed and buried. It is persistently disturbing.

Reformism lets people be comfortable about being comfortable.

The real difference between reformists and revolutionaries is not in their heads but their hearts. Reforms are objectives you try to achieve but revolution is something you are, and it shows in your approach to life. Reformers are so deadly serious and heavy about it. They are the most fearful, frustrated and pessimistic of souls, far-seeing, well aware of what can and cannot be done, full of rules about how to go about things, always talking about change but always stopping where they are.

They want to retain capitalism but clean it up, which is like shaking hands with a clenched fist. They want to avoid violence without admitting that the status quo is maintained by violence. They desire improvements but do not wish to be involved in the struggle against evil and wickedness in high places. They want the church to be strong, but refuse to examine the contention that the church of Jesus cannot co-exist with the priorities of Western civilization. Reformers limp from one conference to another with their Rennies of resolutions and their Elastoplast statements to stick over the blood. Reform is a sad, heavy, desperate, pessimistic business, full of the burden of its terrible responsibilities.

But revolution is a new life which you can actually experience. Nothing is more responsible or more serious, but it is something that is bubbling in you now, not just a promise of something that might happen. Have you ever studied those pictures of the children in Soweto in the demonstration of 1976? Laughing! Of course, they screamed and ran when the police bullets thudded into them, or the dogs tore at their flesh, or the teargas rolled towards them, but their overall mood was one of exultation. And it is infectious: it spreads. Revolution erupts into a celebration of a freedom that is in your heart and will be in your society.

The atmosphere in the prison attached to John Vorster Square Police Station in Johannesburg is not conducive to gaiety. The place is designed to cut you off from the world, to block you by bars in every direction (even the light wells have bars between you and the sky) and the attitude of the police is cruel, callous, hateful. The place is filthy. No one cares.

One day I was being taken by my guard from an interrogation session back to a cell, shouting and banging on the bars to attract the man with the keys at each change of floor or change of section. 'Hek!' (meaning 'Gate!') is the constant shout that echoes down the prison passages. Suddenly, we rounded a corner, and there was my friend Aubrey Mokoena being marched along with his guard, in the opposite direction. For a microsecond pause each one of us calculated if there was any reason why we should not recognize one another and decided there was not, and then shouted in delight, threw our arms round one another, and burst into torrents of quick conversation (Aubrey is incapable of talking slowly anyway). In a flash the gloom had been ripped out of John Vorster and a clean gust of lively revolution tore through the place. Our guards, used to handling submissive prisoners, or snarling prisoners, could not handle this situation of exultant prisoners who were clearly motivated by something quite different. Then they hauled us away from one another and marched us to our separate cells. But the air was cleaner and I slept like a child.

There is an exultancy about the commitment to a revolution bigger than yourself which bursts into exuberance, even if your friends are also in chains, and buoys you up even in the face of possible death. I do not think that reformers would feel that way over a campaign for blacks to use white toilets.

Professor J. Moltmann was right when he wrote: 'Freedom needs more than to be realized: it must be celebrated' (*Theology and Joy*, SCM Press 1973, p. 45). If you are born again to see a new kingdom and recognize that the new-birth life of God on earth really does roll everything over, life becomes incomparably different. When you meet the ordinary grassroots people in whom revolution is happening, with their determination, their confidence, their courage, their unquestioned assurance of victory, something happens to you. When you share in the plans and activity of people who are in touch with the actual political alertness of the masses, you sense that your fingers are on the pulse of God's liberating activity. Revolution is an experience of commitment which reaches out and sets you down in the kingdom-liberation business at whatever cost, and it is in the environment of revolution that you find love, joy, faith, hope and peace.

If we are to take Jesus seriously when he calls us to make disciples for the kingly rule of God on earth, we are called to such a thoroughgoing change in the priorities of this life that we are caught up in a revolution. That is clearly so in South Africa, and South Africa is an eyepiece to the Western world.

From Reform to Revolution

A commitment to reform, however sincerely it may be expressed, is a commitment to keep things fundamentally the same. The commitment to the one who 'makes all things new' is revolution.

7

From Reconciliation to Struggle

Flying down valleys in the dark is not a good recipe for seeing where you are going at nearly two hundred miles an hour but it is the only way for illegal flyers to avoid being picked up on the radar. Because you are so low it has to be dark, for even a person surprised by your approach could look up and read your registration letters. The trick is to take off just before dawn when enough light has smudged over the eastern horizon to sketch in the misty outline of the hills and to follow the valleys until you are well away.

Horst and I pushed the aircraft out of the hangar into the pre-dawn darkness and I leant inside and yanked on the hand brake, oleos mushing a little and her wings wobbling in that ungainly fashion they have on the ground. We pushed the car into the hangar, rolled the doors closed, climbed into the aircraft, all set, brakes on, the prop groaned and fired on its first kick and I let her roll slowly between the hangars and down the perimeter track flicking the lights from time to time to avoid running into the rough.

There was not a peep of an incoming aircraft on the radio and not a sign of life amongst the other parked aircraft, but somewhere a watchman would be looking, unless he was asleep, so Horst kept his head down in case. We swung into the wind, ran up, chopped switches, trickled on to the runway and eased up the throttle. I wondered what Horst was thinking as we bored into the noisy darkness of the runway and then 'left the country' in such a definite way. It was suddenly quieter and smoother as the Cessna put her weight into her wings and the motor settled into its travelling snarl. The dim gleam of dawning set the city in silhouette on the skyline as we hugged the ground for the distant border. You can know the country well from a few thousand feet following a compass course but it is quite different at a few hundred feet when the course is set by the curves of the hills and the compass follows you. We had no alternative to keeping below the line of hills until we had passed beyond radar range, for the South African Defence Force jets could be on to us in ten minutes if they were apprised. By the time Mother Sun had climbed into her own we were well away and rode a little higher.

Horst had no passport (the security police had added it to their collection during his detention) and hardly any possessions to leave the land of his birth and begin life in the world outside. He did not even have a bag which would have attracted attention when he left his house so I lent him mine and he stuffed his few things into it as we flew. I suspect that the desperate loneliness of exile began to hit him whilst we were still over South African soil, although neither of us spoke of it. I never did know what he had done, or why it was that he found this urgency to leave; it was not necessary for me to know. We had gone to supper a few nights before and behind the clatter of the restaurant he had told me that his situation had suddenly become very serious and he must leave as soon as possible. Neither of us knew the escape routes which were spoken of in the press so we made one there and then over the pizzas.

We approached the border at a normal height and on a normal course from airport to airport, but once over we dropped away again and followed a river bed and a line of low hills to the field I had selected near a small remote village. We did not dare attract too much attention so we flew low over the end and it looked all right, but when we came in for a text-book short landing, flaps dangling round our ankles, bags of power ready, prop in its finest cut, I could see mud flying as we touched and knew there was a patch of sticky wetness under the grass that was reaching for us. Stick in my crotch, up flaps, and suddenly we were safe, idling along dry ground as firm as Jan Smuts airport.

We jumped out, pushed the aircraft back to the very edge of the field to give me maximum room for take-off.

'I can't wait.'

'No, you go.'

'Go well.'

Full throttle against the brakes, flaps far down, let everything go, the 182 hit me in the middle of the back and leapt into the air well clear of the mud and shot up into the sky. I rolled over and dived down over Horst to wave goodbye and climbed away waggling wings as he strolled down the track to find a road to find a bus with seven thousand miles to go to Europe.

Coming back was easy. I kept very low and crossed the border in an area I knew was depopulated, calling at a South African town where I had every right to be and spending the day on legitimate business, but I was back in the office next morning. At the staff meeting Beyers Naudé announced that Horst had not come to work and it was thought that he had gone to visit his sister. One of the secretaries later came to my room, swore me to secrecy and whispered that she thought perhaps Horst had left the country, but nothing must be said until we knew he was safely away.

I kept my mouth shut. I had taken illegal liberties with someone's aircraft. Illegally failed to file a flight plan, twice crossed the border illegally, illegally taken someone out of the country without any papers, landed in another country illegally and illegally falsified several entries in log books. You can be sure I kept my mouth shut. This catalogue of crime never troubled my conscience at all. I was only concerned that I should not be found out. So I kept silence.

But I thought of Horst setting off down that dusty track towards Europe with my flight bag slung across his shoulders. Months later the bag came back to me and I have it now in this room where I am writing eight years later, myself an exile.

Does it seem strange to you that someone nurtured in the strictest rectitude of non-conformist righteousness with a high regard for law and order should so deliberately break the law?

The apostle Paul made a statement in his letter to the Christians of Rome which has sometimes sent a ripple of concern through Christians who have found themselves in conflict with the state. 'You must obey all governing authorities. Since all government comes from God the civil authorities were appointed by God so anyone who resists authority is rebelling against God's decision and such an act is bound to be punished' (Romans 13.1f.). This is puzzling. Paul himself was in frequent conflict with the authorities, had been in chains and imprisoned before he wrote this, and spent the four or five following years in custody. Peter, John, Paul, Silas and many other early Christians were jailed. Jesus, Stephen, James the brother of John, and James the brother of Jesus, Peter and Paul himself were all executed judicially. For two thousand years Christians have frequently found themselves in opposition to the authorities despite this injunction by Paul to obey them.

Paul slips the answer into verse seven of this chapter. 'Give any government official *what he has a right to ask*' – whether it be tax, fear or honour. But no state officer has the right to command obedience to dictates which are against the Law of God. Peter and John expressed it boldly in their defence against the Sanhedrin, the Jewish council which sought to silence them for continuing to pursue the way of Jesus. 'You must judge whether in God's eyes it is right to listen to you and not to God. We cannot promise to stop proclaiming what we have seen and heard' (Acts 4.19).

It was not a new notion. Isaiah had written centuries earlier: 'do not call conspiracy all that this people calls conspiracy; do not fear what they fear; do not be afraid of them. It is the Lord God Almighty whom we must hold in veneration, Him you must fear, Him you must dread ' (Isa. 8.12–13).

Where Christians believe a contention exists between the governing authorities and the ways of God they must be obedient to God's jurisdiction even though such an act is 'bound to be punished' by the state, and even if family and friends will suffer in that cause.

In a country where the laws are evil a person must break the laws to do good. The apartheid society, which sets out its commandments to establish an inhuman and ungodly regime by force must inevitably be challenged in every possible way by those who are seeking to overcome evil with good and this means that government demands which they have no right to make will be ignored or broken, and the minions of the state

93

who seek to enforce those evil laws will be challenged, ignored, or overcome.

Christians in Southern Africa who believe the promises and the warnings of the scripture, and in behaviour seek to follow them, walk with those the authorities condemn. It is disgraceful to be law abiding when the law is inhuman and ungodly. We must throw off its restraints with determination and glee and walk into freer air, even if it is dangerous.

The necessity of Christian antagonism to the law in the liberation struggle is apparent if we consider the conflicting convictions which our people hold. Slipping into someone else's skin for a moment enables us to see the essential problem of South Africa: we all think we are right, from our own point of view.

Consider *the Afrikaner*. Dr D. F. Malan, a clergyman who was the first Prime Minister of the Nationalist government in 1948, said:

Our history is the greatest masterpiece of the centuries. We hold this nationhood as our due for it was given to us by the architect of the universe ... indeed, the history of the Afrikaner reveals a will and a determination which makes one feel that Afrikanerdom is not the work of men but the creation of God.

In his struggle against the domination of British Imperialism the Afrikaner was convinced that he was under God's guidance. He fought to obtain the freedom of his birthright and that struggle which began in the quest for a peaceful pastoral world has led him to grasp for proficiency in statecraft, industry, commerce, and world relationships. It is only due to the blessing of God that the Afrikaner has been able to maintain the Nationalist Party in control of Parliament for a third of a century and thus enable unprecedented progress to be made throughout the land. Dr J. D. Vorster, the clergyman brother of a former Prime Minister, wrote in the South African *Sunday Times* (8 November 1970):

Our only guide is the Bible. Our policy and outlook on life are based on the Bible. We firmly believe the way we interpret it is right. . . . We are right and will continue to follow the way the Bible teaches.

The Afrikaner has a high sense of responsibility towards the Bantu and would still support the following words of Dr Malan:

The difference in colour is merely the physical manifestation of two irreconcilable ways of life, between barbarism and civilization, between heathenism and christianity.

The Dutch Reformed Church set out its own position at its General Synod in 1974 (*Human Relations and the South African Scene in the Light of Scripture*):

The Dutch Reformed Church is only too well aware of the serious problems in respect of inter-people, inter-racial and inter-human relationships in South Africa. It seeks to achieve the same ideals of social justice, human rights and self determination for peoples and individuals, based on God's word as do other churches . . . If the Dutch Reformed church does differ from other churches . . . there is no difference in ideals and objectives, but merely disagreement on the best methods of achieving these ideals.

Different dangers now surround us, for the forces of Liberalism, Communism, and Terrorism abound. Wittingly or not, churchmen, students and blacks are being lured by the agents of Russian Imperialism to sow seeds of spiritual weakness in our society and destroy us. Only by adhering to the strong Christian lead given by our government not only to our own country but to all the countries of the subcontinent can we be sure of marching forward together towards a peaceful and prosperous future in which all men might share.

The *English-speaking South African*, has a different approach. A quotation from earlier years will still receive much acclaim:

Whatever there is to give grace, dignity, progress, and security to life is based on the development and achievements of the European, and in him lies the guarantee of the future. Surrender him to the teeming masses who are being raised by him, and on whom those masses are dependent for continued progress, and the future of western civilisation is surrendered (J. J. McCord, *South African Struggle*, Bussy, p. 523).

More recently some Americans have written words which would be widely accepted:

There is no better hope for South Africa and for the world at large than the ascendency of the moderates. . . . As long as blacks can see that they are moving toward the ideals of justice, dignity, equality and freedom, they will work with the system and not listen to the call of arms (Gann and Dingan, *South Africa: War? Revolution? Peace?*, Tafelberg, p. 85).

Professor D. Hobart Houghton believed:

Most thinking white people would agree that there are individual Africans of outstanding merit every wit as competent as any white. They believe however that a dynamic modern industrial society requires policy to be directed by people possessed of certain rare qualities of leadership, enterprise and initiative, and that these qualities, despite the proved adaptability of Africans, are more abundant among white South Africans than among black, because of the latter's cultural history and social institutions.

Clutching a Bible and hurrying off to a prayer meeting, *the Pietist* has no time for such considerations, for if people would only give their hearts to Christ none of these problems would arise. If only the churches would stick to spiritual matters and keep out of politics!

The saboteur carefully cuddling a limpet mine on to the cold steel side of a petrol tank containing half a million rands worth of fuel is convinced he is risking death for freedom. Reared in a Christian home and a Christian school he learnt early of the fatherhood of God and the brotherhood of man but has known that he is different because he is black. His home is a shack; there are a hundred in his school class; he grows up in poverty, malnourished, subjected. Deaths happen daily from disease, neglect, ignorance and stabbings in the dark. Pieces of white man's paper control his life. Life for him and his friends who have been arrested, banned, restricted or killed for political reasons, is persecution against which he does not have and cannot get the vote, the money, the position, the power, the influence, or the respect to bring change.

But there is a manliness in him which comes from the godliness which made him and he is determined to follow the steps of King David in the Old Testament, and of the Saxon, and the American, and the Afrikaner, and reach out to liberate himself by fighting for his freedom, and destroying the powers that prevent it. He creeps away under the fence and back into the anonymity of the townships with the sky erupting in flames and smoke behind him, exulting in the fact that he has delivered a blow for justice and liberty.

We the people of South Africa declare for all our country and the world to know: That South Africa belongs to all who live in it, black and white, and that no government can justly claim authority unless it is based on the will of all the people; that our people have been robbed of their birthright to land, liberty and peace by a form of government founded on injustice and inequality; that our country will never be prosperous or free until all our people live in brotherhood, enjoying equal rights and opportunities; that only a democratic state, based on the will of all the people, can secure to all their birthright without distinction of colour, race, sex or belief; and therefore, we the people of South Africa, black and white together – equals, countrymen and brothers – adopt this *Freedom Charter*. And we pledge ourselves to strive together, sparing neither strength nor courage, until the democratic changes here set out have been won.

People hold these and other opinions with a depth and a sincerity which is gravely hurt by the gross insensibility of everyone else, which they ascribe to stubborn stupidity, or hellish hypocrisy, and to which they react in hurt aloofness or with a snarl. Because each group is convinced that in God's sight it alone has the seeds of survival there is no hope of survival; when each group advocates its way to peace it is inflaming war; attempts to promote friendship provoke enmity: for these views are irreconcilable. We seem to be doomed because we are all too damned good. So we must dig deeper.

When people clash we can distinguish different categories of conflicts. There are clashes of personality or temperament when there is little to choose between the rights or wrongs of the case and the reconciler's task is to enable people to see one another's point of view, make allowances, and come to a common position. In such a case it is desirable for someone to retain a neutral role, to attend equally to both viewpoints and bring them to a centre, and refuse to take sides.

Clashes of principle are of a different nature for where there is a confrontation between right and wrong, or good and evil, or a struggle against injustice or oppression or lies, Christians can adopt no central or neutral role, but must take sides firmly and definitely in the struggle and throw their weight entirely upon one effort only. You cannot reconcile God and mammon, or seek to make a case for those who embrace wrong. You must fight for one and against the other with every ounce of your strength, and there can be no neutral position, for permitting evil to continue is aiding it instead of resisting it, like a person passing on a deadly disease.

The South African conflict lies in this second category and Christians must be totally involved in the struggle for liberation in which we perceive the pressure of God's kingly rule. It is a struggle against fascist totalitarianism, against capitalist exploitation, against dehumanization, against deportation, against detention without trial and death and illegal war and oppression in all its forms. There is no way for Christians to reconcile their faith with such evil which must be destroyed as part of the Christian witness.

Professor P. V. Pistorius wrote words a generation ago which the passing years have only confirmed:

> If one group regards itself as the nation ... and its own interests as being paramount ... and if that group in doing so lays claim to divine aid and divine protection, it has in fact degraded its concept of divinity to the status of a tribal

god, and in that case its tribal god will have to contend with other tribal gods. If a church explicitly or by implication becomes an accessory to this it must lose its cosmic and Christian character (*No Further Talk*, CNA, p. 40).

This is precisely the position which prompted an African in the height of a political rally in Durban to cry out:

> Today we are living under three hundred years of European domination of this land . . . these people here are Christians but they eat people . . . if they represent God then they represent a false God. And if God is like that then God is no good for Africa. If God says my children must be looked after but your children must starve . . . the God of these people, he can't be our God at all.

The preamble to the Act to introduce a new Constitution for the Republic of South Africa in 1983 begins with the words:

> In humble submission to Almighty God, who controls the destinies of peoples and nations, who gathered our forebears together from many lands and gave them this their own, who has guided them from generation to generation, who has wondrously delivered them from the dangers that beset them, we declare that we are conscious of our responsibility towards God and man; and are convinced of the necessity of standing united and of pursuing the following national goals: To uphold Christian values and civilized norms etc. etc.

When a government with the record and the policy of the South African government declares that these are done as a result of its Christian principles that is not sin which could be forgiven, but heresy* which must be stamped out. It is the task of Christians to be totally unreconciled with this evil, to make clear that there is no possibility of them attempting to adjust or normalize it, but only to abolish and exterminate it. And where men and women and boys and girls under the pressure of the jurisdiction of God's kingdom which is built into human society rise up in protest and seek to be rid of this wrong it is the

*See John W. Gruchy, 'Towards a Confessing Church: The Implications of a Heresy', *Epworth Review*, Vol. 10, no. 3, pp. 23–32.

Christian's task to become totally committed and engaged in that struggle.

There is a common idea amongst whites, and in the West, that talking is better than fighting, which it certainly is: but people must be very careful when they say that we must go on talking at all cost. At the cost of injustice? Must we go on talking while others pay the cost in suffering? Shall we pursue talks at Church Conferences or share-holders meetings or political debating societies and say that this is better than having a war, whilst people suffer and starve and are killed by the South African system because we talk to avoid entering the struggle? There comes a time when talk of reconciliation, or of maintaining peace and order, is used as an instrument of violence, as a tool to perpetuate the continuation of exploitation and oppression, and that time has long since passed in the case of South Africa.

The most famous photograph to come out of the Soweto demonstration in 1976 was of Hector Peterson, the first black youth to be killed by police bullets on that day, as he was carried to a nearby car by a friend with his sister screaming in horror alongside. We reprinted that photograph on the cover of the Christian Institute journal *Pro Veritate* and printed alongside it a quotation from the Prime Minister John Vorster:

> The Government will not be intimidated, and orders have been given to maintain order at all cost (House of Assembly, Cape Town, 18 June 1976).

The advocates of apartheid have had every opportunity in the last thirty years to put their case fairly and squarely in every court that exists in our country and the rest of the world: Judicial, ecclesiastical, academic, political, economic, and in the realm of organized labour. They have been judged and been found guilty in every sphere and the time for talking is passed, the time for struggle has come.

It is not necessary for those who are seeking the Christian way on earth to return once more to the arguments over the abolition of slavery, or the suffragette movement, or the provision of pensions. These battles have been fought and won long since and so has the verbal justification and condemnation of apartheid. The debating is done, the judgment is pronounced, the sentence must be carried out, and a new life begun.

Jesus did not adopt a neutral position but took sides unequivocally with the outcasts and oppressed. Reconciliation demands the pursuit of irreconciliation with all oppressive forces whether of government or business or thought and whether in South Africa or the rest of the world. Demonstrative acts of irreconciliation with wrong are essential parts of the commitment to good.

> New Testament Eschatology is a call to arms, a summons not to be content with the existing situation of oppression but to take sides with the oppressed and the poor and subsequently for the new humanity and a new world (Allan Boesak, *Farewell to Innocence*, Kampen, p. 114).

There is only one struggle in South Africa and that is the struggle of the people for liberation and it is our task to join in that struggle. The struggle is not to find ways in which to talk to the South African government: they will always turn such strategies to their advantage. The struggle is to find ways in which we may compel the South African government to talk with us. There is no other struggle except the struggle to be rid of oppression and bring all the representatives of South Africa to the round table to decide our future together.

Liberation is a pre-requisite of reconciliation not the result of it. It is only after our peoples' battle for freedom has been won that we shall be able to sit down together and work out what freedom means. Our first task is to win the liberty to do that.

It comes as something of a shock to Christians who have been nurtured in the belief that they should be 'gentle and humble in heart' to discover that the words of struggle, conflict, battle, and fight, become imperatives to be obeyed. When we are called to be in conflict with evil our desire to avoid dissension is a temptation which must be overcome. Indoctrination to make a virtue of docility, or to confuse the pursuit of peace with submission to evil, are two of the wicked and cunning techniques of the 'principalities and powers'. Many people are not only resistant to fighting against specific wrongs but seem to have a principle that they should not struggle against anything. It is the laissez faire attitude by which many people indicate their acquiescence in their own oppression. Very often when people say, 'it will work itself out', or 'it will all come right in the end', or 'you won't get anywhere by upsetting people', or 'grin and bear it', they are simply giving themselves a justification for getting out of their responsibility to the struggle.

When people do this about societies' needs and claim it is a Christian principle to avoid such a struggle they are on most dangerous ground. Jesus was a deliberate provoker of conflict against those who promoted evil, and he used the most evocative language and action to break through the protective shell with which these 'hypocrites' shielded themselves. Reading the stories in the Gospels we study a man in conflict and confrontation particularly with the rich and the religious, and by his own decision and act. He was not pushed into it. Whilst the 'common people' heard him gladly many of the elite did not; it is equally certain that the elite did not hear the common people gladly. They still don't.

This belligerent attitude to evil, the concept of an enemy to be fought and destroyed, the spreading of the gospel against the active and subtle opposition is one that we do not like; many of us feel we should apologise for being *against* something and spend much time and energy avoiding the possibility. But against evil is one of the places we must be, boots and all, 'not counting the cost'.

As the commitment to the struggle for liberation clarified and enlivened the situation for me I had to apply it to the resources that I used most of all: words. It was my job to speak and to write and those words had to become part of the struggle against darkness and for light, against oppression and for liberation, against confusion and deceit and for simplicity and commitment, against despair and disillusion and for enlightenment and hope. There were many ways in which it would have been so easy to have taken a Christian interest in things other than the struggle, by specializing in something which was of peripheral concern, but that would have been like the disciples who went to sleep when Jesus left them with a job to do.

Sometimes there is a loneliness in the struggle, a sadness at being separated and rejected from people you would love to work with more closely, there is the anguish of trying to work out whether a negative reaction is due to your ineptness in putting it across or due to the message itself, and the frustrations and impatience which build up when people try to divert you into quieter channels 'for your own good'. All of them are problems which Jesus knew and overcame. It is necessary for the trumpet to have a *certain* sound if it is indeed to awaken the sleepless, to rouse the dead, and to make people open their eyes and see what Jesus sees. Fog signals and warning sirens are not designed for people to like the tone but to alert them to danger and direct them into the safe course.

Those whose business is words must use them as part of the struggle.

For the oppressed and dispossessed the struggle is a fact of life for which there is no escape from the state machinery which enforces their subjugation to a life of repression and poverty. It is a struggle for everything: work, income, food, roof, medicine, or a patch of land. It is a struggle for political expression at illegal meetings with illegal literature and illegal people. It is a struggle against hidden cameras, bugged telephones, informers, whispers, against censored mail, against jail, beatings, torture and sleepless days and nights of interrogation or the frustrating boredom of detentions.

For me, commitment to the struggle meant a constantly increasing role as a supporter for the people who were in the front line. Money, transport, food, equipment, encouragement, consultancy, literature, ideas, sounding board, go-between: the struggle goes on and it is too soon to tell it all in detail.

When I was banned in October 1977 it made things easier in some ways because there was no necessity to keep up an above board life. If your concerns are mostly underground it is easier if you are prevented from doing anything overground, and the banning order clearly restricted that. Like hundreds of other people with banning orders I was confined to the Municipal area in which I lived – in Johannesburg; I could not attend schools or universities or factories; black residential areas of any sort were prohibited ground for me: I was not allowed to speak, write or prepare anything for publication; nor was I allowed to attend meetings or social gatherings of any sort if more than two people were there; and I was not allowed to meet anybody else who was banned at all. The struggle meant that you broke every one of these orders not once but constantly. Inevitably, our extended family, which included our friends and comrades, became involved in the whole situation co-operatively, protectively or operationally. And then a new dimension appeared.

After all peaceful means of political action had been closed to it in 1960 the African National Congress had established Umkhonto we Sizwe (the Spear of the Nation), a military wing which would operate in the field of guerrilla and sabotage activities directed against the centres of oppressive power. The MK units operate in complete secrecy and isolation from anything else as is clearly desirable. It was not my part of the struggle although I fully realized that there must be those about me who were involved.

From the early 1950s I had been a pacifist believing that war was intrinsically wrong because it seldom achieved its objectives, and if it did it achieved them at such great cost that other methods ought to obviate. It was not the experience of living throughout the Nazi blitz on London that convinced me of this, but the total devastation inflicted upon Europe and upon Tokyo, Hiroshima and Nagasaki. I did not believe and I do not believe that was permissible.

The violence in the South African situation was of a different nature. Despite the stream of propaganda, I was well aware that the violence in South Africa came from the white government and not from the black oppressed peoples. I went through a long process of moral and theological struggle within my own head on these issues which demanded that I became acquainted with the sufferings and opinions of the people who endured the violence of our oppressive system. To say simply 'I don't approve of violence' is no valid reason for rejecting it. The oppressed people do not approve of violence either but they are in a situation in which violence is forced upon them and in which self-defence becomes a fact of survival.

I enjoyed a fair amount of target shooting at one time but on the first occasion I had to apply my skills against a wild cat that was killing the chickens on the mission farm, I discovered there was a difference between the decisiveness with which I shot it and the squeamishness which made me very glad that someone else picked up the twitching corpse by its tail. In the wider sphere I came to realize I could not let my revulsion of violence deny my recognition that it had a role on earth.

How can white people, whether they live in South Africa, Europe or North America know what it is like to live in Crossroads, Soweto or unheard of and unpronounceable places like Gqogqora or Thabanchu? Life in the townships or the Homelands is not a slightly downgraded version of life in an affluent suburb, but something quite different and unimaginable which commands difficult words like experiential and situational even to grasp the concept.

The courage and suffering of the women at Greenham Common has excited the interest and concern of thousands through frequent newspaper and television exposure, but there are hundreds of thousands of people in South Africa (and millions in the world) who live in such conditions throughout their lives. They are born in them, they study for matric in them, they court their mates and make love in them, they rear their families and die in them and cannot conquer the elements because the circumstances of life compel them to a wet and muddy and cold, or a dry and dusty and sweated, defeat. What is it like to be in a situation where such furniture as there is must be moved to enable people to put blankets on the floor to sleep? How can you sit in judgment upon men in the condemned cells in 'Beverley Hills' on the higher slopes of the koppie behind Pretoria Central Prison, with the clang of jailer's keys, the constant shouting and the cruelty, and the prisoners' prayers and singing? How can you possibly enter the decision made by a black youth who no longer can stomach the poverty, the ill-education, the crowded nature of life, the injustice and brutality and humiliation to which parents are submitted, and who voluntarily becomes a homeless exile in order to fight for a homeland in which there are no exiles?

It is insensitive for the elite to speak of their rejection of violence when they themselves have not endured the constant hurt from the enforcers of a system of institutionalized violence, the endless domination of officials, permits, approvals, permissions, arguments, the submissiveness to survival which cramps the human spirit, and the constant watch for pass raids, informers, or the swift onrush of police with their dogs and gas and guns. To insist that others must first subscribe to a non-violent principle before you speak to them is yourself to do violence to the apprehension of reality which is experienced by oppressed people. Only the grass roots understand the reality of the situation as they themselves experience it and we must defend that right and learn from that understanding.

There is all the difference in the world between the violence of the South African government and the violence of the ANC. Our government existed by enforcing itself upon millions, it had violently removed over three million from their homes in fulfilment of its policies without consultation or the consent of those involved, it incarcerated hundreds of thousands every year, had shot thousands in cold blood, and the secret demise of detainees in the hands of the Security Police was a regular occurrence. On the other hand, the MK units over the years had made hundreds of attacks upon the system and *only in a handful of cases had anyone been killed or injured.* Indeed, there were many times when MK agents had endangered themselves by the precautions they took not to harm the civilian population. It was abundantly clear that anyone who worked for the oppressive system thereby put themselves in a different category.

I could see all the arguments but it was a matter of academic concern about something which happened to other people. Then one night a friend who I knew quite well explained to me that sometimes MK operatives were injured and needed immediate assistance before they were able to return to their units. It meant providing safe accommodation, obtaining the agreement of nurses and doctors to care for wounded men (which involved declaring my own involvement), securing of medical supplies, furnishings, transport, and other matters. Would I do this?

The kingdom of God will not come on earth, nor liberation in South Africa, by slaughtering all the opposition in a war of devastation and destruction: but sometimes the sources of oppression need to be overcome by force and Christians who are committed to the struggle must not flinch from it. I said Yes.

I never had the slightest quiver about breaking the law when that law prevented the work of liberation from proceeding and used to muse upon the precedents in idle moments. When the court in Jerusalem sought to ban the early Christians one of their leaders, Gamaliel, had these words of warning: 'If this enterprise, this movement of theirs, is of human origin it will break up of its own accord; but if it does in fact come from God you will not be able to destroy them but you might find yourselves fighting against God' (Acts 5.39).

On those illegal flights to drop comrades off in neighbouring countries when their lives were endangered, I remembered what happened to Paul when he was trapped by his opponents.

'To make sure of killing him they kept watch on the gates day and night but when it was dark his friends took him and let him down from the top of the city wall lowering him in a basket' (Acts 9.25).

Sack or Cessna, what's the difference?

8

From Church Institutions
to Ecclesia Groups

South Africa is an intensely religious country. It always was.
The African people have been religious from the earliest records,
and though the passing centuries may have redirected their
mythologies, the religious nature remains. Today there are a
quarter of a million Moslems, half a million Hindus, and over
twenty million Christians, covering every racial and cultural
group, every denomination, and thousands of indigenous sects.

Whatever else may be said about the rulers of South Africa,
they are one of the most avowedly Christian governments in the
world, many of whose members are loyal and regular supporters
of their local church. The South African Government has invited so much invective by the cruelty and callousness of its acts,
that we forget these are most respectable, correct and proper
Christian gentlemen, whose manners and attitudes are the same
as those which appear around the Cabinet Room of number 10,
Downing Street, the boardroom of any Western company, or
any church committee.

It is very easy to engage members of the Security Police in
religious conversation during interrogation, because most are
sensitive to the accusation that they are not Christians. One of
the ploys they used against me was unnerving at the time but
interesting in retrospect. I was stripped naked, handcuffed and
they then brought in nearly all the staff from the ninth and tenth
floors of the Security Police offices at John Vorster Square to
surround me. Those that could not pack inside the room, went
into adjacent offices and stood on desks to glare through the

clear glass in the top of the partitions. I was deluged with insults, questions and tirades all of which embroidered the theme: How can you as a Christian support the ANC, be a terrorist, be a commie, and put your family in peril? 'We are Christians, but you are not.' Once you understand their twisted mentality, you realize that from their point of view they are being completely sincere. They have been indoctrinated from their mother's milk to believe that their attitudes are Christian and correct, even if the whole world is against them. Having learnt from previous encounters that it is impossible to argue in such a situation, I sought to present a dignified mein, reminiscent of Queen Victoria or Paul Kruger, me dressed only in my handcuffs.

As they all trouped out, each one delivered a parting blast in the vein of 'May God bring you to your senses', and the door was shut. One man remained alone to perform the next act, a well-known thug. He began by saying: 'I am *not* a Christian', and proceeded to attack me, pulling me off my feet, and dragging me around the room by my hair. It was extremely difficult not to retaliate, but I knew they would like nothing better than to shoot me.

Implicit in this whole exercise, and behind all the psychological manipulation employed, was a desperate desire within the Security Police to maintain that we are a Christian country, with Christian standards, and cannot accept any criticisms from other Christians. Un-Christian things must be done out of sight and behind the backs of authority. Hidden by the hypocrisy, underneath the psychological games they play with us, beneath their sad expressions of regret at the necessity of using these tragic means to defend the ways of Western civilization, under the appalling caricature of Christianity to which they adhere, is a recognition of the genuine thing.

I have strong feelings about the Security Branch and the Government, but I do not blame them for being hypocrites. It is the leaders of the churches who condone and support this hypocrisy, who recognize the heretical beliefs and continue to accept them, that must bear full responsibility. To use the apocalyptic language which so many of them love: when the trumpet of the Lord shall sound, it could well be that many of the thugs in the police and army will go into Heaven with blood on their hands for which they have been forgiven, but many church leaders with their white ties and clerical collars will go protesting into Hell crying: 'Lord, Lord, when did we do anything to hurt you?' and hear the divine retort: 'I never knew you.'

It is customary to classify churches inside South Africa according to their attitude to the doctrine of apartheid. The white Dutch Reformed Church, home of the Afrikaner Nationalists, bore and nurtures the apartheid policy. Most of their theologians argue that separate development is necessary and justified, if it is implemented in accordance with the Christian principles of justice and love. It is a heresy to the younger Dutch Reformed churches – the black daughter churches – a judgment which the Christian world endorses. Both the Protestant and Catholic 'English speaking' churches have been constantly critical of it. The Independent charismatic churches in black and white communities normally refrain from any political statements.

This traditional analysis is far from satisfactory on several counts. It ignores the fact that most churches in South Africa meet in racially divided congregations, citing historical, geographical, linguistic or cultural reasons. We inherited a society which was divided into White, Black, Asian and Coloured Group Areas before we were able to be consulted and inevitably those who attend the church on the corner will be with people of the same language, colour, ethnic background and culture. It is also true for schools, cinemas, sportsfields and bottlestores.

Bringing the practice of the so-called multi-racial churches into harmony with their expressed policy and belief is a major task of liberation requiring definite decisions and actions which few churches will be willing to accept until they are committed to fight for liberation in their own membership. If they really believe the kingdom of God is the answer, many do little about it at the moment. 'The Government might not like it, and the people would not understand, you see.'

Ignorance, prejudice and fear of government action or congregational pressure abound in the anti-apartheid churches. Very many ministers, church leaders and committees are governed, not by the love of Christ, but by fear of the Government's heel or the financier's toe.

One congregation in which I worked invited a black minister to preach in their church for the first time, and despite several objections there was a packed house. Two days later I met a member who regretted her absence but had heard it was a good service, and that he was a good preacher and spoke very good English. She asked if she could state a personal question.

'Is it true he stayed in your house?'

'Yes, visiting preachers usually do. His wife stayed with us too.'

'Yes, well, was it all right?' I said: 'Do you mean was it legal?'

'Oh no. I mean did they behave properly?' 'You mean in the home?'

'Yes, in front of the children. Can he use a knife and fork?'

Multiracial statements by church conferences should not obscure the fact that there is little multiracial experience amongst church members who have lived and worked with people of other races all their lives – in their kitchen and work places. White Methodists and Anglicans behave towards black people exactly the same as white members of the Dutch Reformed Church: good and bad, kind or cruel, paternalistic or human.

Analysing the churches on the basis of their official policies also conceals the existence of opposition groups in all churches. Behind the declaration of the Methodist Church of South Africa that it is 'one and undivided', there have been decades of struggle to fit the reality to the words. Every political, financial and social skill has been employed to delay every step of advance and it is only now in the middle of the 1980s that the church has begun to give serious consideration in its legislation to the enactment of non-racial churches at the local level. It is simply unwilling to put its beliefs into practice, and a similar picture applies to most churches. The comment of a leading Anglican layman in the diocese of Johannesburg when Bishop Desmond Tutu's passport was taken away was: 'Thank God! Every time he goes overseas he costs us a million in lost investment.'

The Roman Catholics have advanced further and more

rapidly than any other church in recent years in their protestations, their thinking and their action, but the resistance within that church is strong and frightening. Bishop Mandla Zwane has written:

> History, I fear, when assessing the impact of the church on the political realities of today, where a dominant white minority impose their will on a preponderently large majority of blacks, will come to the conclusion that the same racist attitudes pervaded Church and State. If the hierarchy is not condemned for its actual support of the structures of oppression it will easily be accused of a play-safe policy. (*A Man for all People*, Catholic Institute for International Relations 1983, p. 43).

None of the so-called anti-apartheid churches can claim majority support from its white members, or point to a general enactment of its belief in the life of the local church. The struggle continues.

There is also an increasingly vociferous opposition within the white Dutch Reformed Church. It has always been there, epitomised in Dr C. F. Beyers Naudé who was rejected by the church leaders because of his acceptance of a position in the Christian Institute nearly twenty years ago, but its whispers have hardly been heard against the roar and bombast of Die Kerkbode, the Synods and the leaders and thousands of dominees and elders in the local congregations. Nevertheless the opposition has grown.

During 1982 an Open Letter was sent to the Dutch Reformed Church by 123 (later 148) ministers and theologians which strongly criticized the apartheid policies in the State and in the relations between the white and black churches in the Dutch Reformed Church family. This Open Letter, rejected by the DRC Synod on technical grounds, was followed by another from 38 prominent lay members of the church in the Transvaal.

All churches include large groups which would align themselves with those who practise pietistic or charismatic Mental Removal Schemes upon themselves, and claim that the church should keep totally apart from all political issues. *All* churches are considered by radical political liberationists to suffer varying degrees of hypocrisy and irrelevance.

The real issue facing the churches in South Africa is not the negative repressive apartheid policy but the positive liberation movement, where the dynamics of the kingdom are working out and the jurisdiction of God is being enacted. Judgment is upon the apartheid system which will go; the Liberation Movement is Good News for the people. Thus it is far more helpful if we analyse South African Christians in terms of their attitudes and participation in the liberation struggle. Setting aside the public statements of the churches, what pressures develop amongst the membership of the churches? The picture alters considerably and recognizes lines of agreement and commitment which run through them all.

The first is *the status quo group*. In terms of our earlier discussion, they comprehend Christianity to be a form of civil religion, whose task is to uphold the traditional political and economic principles of the state. This group comprises the great majority of white Christians in all churches. This does not mean that they all hug the Nationalist hustings nor are uncritical of the present structures, but whichever views these people propagate, or Party for which they cast their vote, they believe that admitting blacks to a full democracy now would endanger 'White Western Christian Civilization'; they agree that it is necessary to perpetuate the 'South African way of life' by the force of a strong army; they maintain that blacks must be encouraged to 'emerge from the darkness at their own pace and in their own areas'; and they are petrified by the propaganda of the danger of a total onslaught from 'Terrorists' and 'Russian Imperialism'.

This attitude is exemplified in a letter which was published in a church newspaper during 1983 when the theological justification of apartheid was declared heretical.

Sir,

Recently a resolution was passed by the authorities of the Methodist Church that apartheid be declared a heresy.

I had to search myself to see whether I could honestly align myself to this declaration, knowing that if I couldn't, that I was a heretic.

I know that I am not alone in this dilemma and so I would like to put my point as defence to the judgement already laid upon me.

Separate development means the opposite of integration, which in South Africa means the power being put into the hands of the black man.

In an unsophisticated country with low population density perhaps the black man could cope.

South Africa however, is neither unsophisticated nor sparsely populated. It has a vast infra structure which if it were to break down would cause untold misery, starvation and even death to the vast majority of our black population and to that of our neighbouring states.

History has and is proving that our white population is the only one which can protect and maintain this infra structure for the forseeable future and thereby ensure the growth which will feed future generations.

No Christian would wish the plight of the rural black man in our neighbouring hostile states, who are poor, disillusioned, unfortunate, forgotten, starving people, on our black population in South Africa.

Under the mantle of this infra structure in South Africa the black man gets job opportunities, and with enlightenment, increasing authority and say over his own plight, and the white and black populations can grow symbiotically in this fashion.

This oversimplifies the problem, but the basic alternatives are there. As a white Christian I'd rather have my black Christian friend live and endure apartheid, than die under a fool's paradise of Marxism or a dictatorship introduced by one man, one vote, once again!

Here in South Africa under the dominance and protection of the whites the blacks multiply and flourish better than anywhere else in Africa. Who is to say that the blacks aren't the most cherished of God, put into the protection of white materialists?

I feel that the Church authorities have polarised the minds of the body of Christ by making a stand on this complex delicate problem.

R. T. W. Zingel
Randburg

(From the Methodist newspaper *Dimension*, 3 April 1983)

This *status quo group* runs right across the board from the Dutch Reformed Church to all the English speaking churches to the charismatic Pentecostal and the American-type sects of the well to do. Any of them could have written this twisted racist letter – but hardly any blacks would have done so. The only blacks who support the *status quo* are those who, like whites, feel their economic dependence upon it. This group does *not* assist the Liberation struggle.

The second group to be found across the entire church spectrum are *the cop-out group* who claim that the gospel must not become involved with political and economic issues. In practice this amounts to an acceptance of the *status quo* society. Such people may spend vast amounts of money on highly publicized and well attended conferences, attended by leading world evangelistic figures, but if they are giving their attention solely to personal spiritual concerns they are of no more benefit to the liberation struggle than the Nationalist Party.

Urging people to love one another without urging them to change a society which institutionalizes the separation and selfishness which prevents love is a total cop-out. The over-emphasis on an individualistic concept of piety may use highly religious language and holy practices but it becomes a hybrid, a sort of spiritual masturbation, a substitution experience which releases tension but gives nothing to others and is non-salvific, non-liberationary and oppressive.

Some Christians have fallen into this group without intending to and it is far larger than is realized.

When the Christian Institute was banned and those of the staff who had not already received the distinction were also banned, I was visited by two of the Christian Institute Board members. They apologized for coming together and wished to speak to me separately, because the banning order precluded me from meeting more than one other person at a time. I said that whilst I must obey the banning order in public I had no intention of letting it rule my personal life and invited them to sit down, pointing out that they were the ones with the problem if we were caught together because they would have to decide whether to give evidence against me or not. They sat down somewhat gingerly and began to discuss the situation presented by the banning. My task had been in the preparation of the Christian Institute journal *Pro Veritate*, and in the operation of groups which the Christian Institute supported in the Transvaal, from all of which activities I was now specifically banned. I was full of plans for continued activity.

'No, no', said my friends, 'You have done your part and must not further endanger yourself by continuing to operate in the background. You must leave it to us now.' We're still waiting.

Their convictions remain the same, they pray and study and are concerned, but in practice they are doing nothing because it would be dangerous. As far as the actual liberation struggle is concerned they are as ineffective as if they believed in oppression. Their commitment to spreading the gospel does not include grappling with dangerous political issues, or personal risk. They copped out.

This group does *not* assist the liberation struggle.

The *tokenist group* of Christians expresses itself against apartheid, making statements and resolutions about it, and would genuinely like to see changes in the country, but has failed to make a correct analysis of the cause of the problem and thus its objections are easily pushed into a side channel from which they have no or little effect upon the liberation struggle. It is a common attitude amongst so-called 'liberals' in English, Afrikaans and African churches and is an attitude strongly espoused by those blacks who are more concerned for a place for themselves in whatever system is going rather than in a liberating system for society. They are trying to reform the civil religion but not to replace it.

This is the group that puts great emphasis on putting the church's own house in order, in equalizing the stipends of black and white clergy, putting blacks into positions which were formerly occupied by whites, for agitating for mixed theological seminaries. These are clearly desirable objects but they easily conceal the fact that it is the nature of our society that is wrong not its personnel, as it is the objectives and priorities of the churches that are oppressive not merely the race of their leading officials.

If all racist restrictions and limitations were removed from the churches overnight we would still be faced with a caricature of Christianity. If blacks were given the vote and there was no fundamental change in the nature of our society we should continue to be an oppressive society ruled by the priorities of the wealthy, and people would still need liberating.

This is the essential problem of Zimbabwe: the conditions imposed on the new Government by the Lancaster House Agreement, whilst they admit blacks to citizenship, do not admit the formation of a truly new society. The country is hamstrung, committed to the former capitalist dependency in which there is no liberation, and is still faced with the neccessity of fundamental change.

Several churches have made great strides towards non-racialism but have been so nurtured in the old styles that many blacks who have come to the top are simply embodiments of the old white masterminds, hugging position and prestige to themselves, with not a thought of the kingdom in their heads and no more resemblance to the ways of Jesus than there was in the bad old days. Things are better – but they are not liberating the people of the church in either black or white churches, in the opinion of black and white leaders who *are* liberated and carry these great burdens.

The manner in which the Methodist Conference out-manoeuvred itself on the stipend issue is an illustration of its fudging on the theological and psychological issues. Methodist ministers are paid from local circuit contributions sent through a central church banking system. The new regulations simply declared that the lowest stipend paid in black circuits was the basic stipend for everyone, and that anything extra was a voluntary contribution from the local church. Everything continued exactly as it had before with the black men receiving low and the white men receiving high, except that they attempted to fool themselves that stipends were now equalized, a case which I have heard ex-Presidents argue with the utmost sincerity. There was not the slightest attempt to alter the system to share out stipends equally for this would have challenged the church at its roots.

Tokenists are reformists who have not realized that effecting small cosmetic changes does nothing to alter the structure that lies underneath and requires drastic surgery, which itself will change the outward appearance in due course. Tokenists are rightly concerned with changing personal attitudes, but cannot do a damned thing with it. There is nothing quite so effective in preventing changes of structure in churches or society as putting all the emphasis on personal attitudes without a follow through. My racist attitudes started to come right when I began to work with blacks in the struggle, not by talking about my feelings.

Another sign of tokenism which may be most sincerely held until the person is prised out of captivity by some converting agency, is that of calling upon the Government to change. Since I have been in Europe it has been fascinating to share in the fervour of the anti-missile demonstrations which have swept this continent and its detached island, with millions of people marching to demand that their Governments totally reject the presence of nuclear missiles. To be caught up in these mammoth assemblies is a deeply moving experience, highly impressive – and utterly ineffective. Polite demonstrations which request Governments to change their minds may have a conscientizing role on the participants but they will not liberate the Governments.

We learnt this in South Africa through the Passive Resistance Campaigns which swept the country a generation ago. Thousands of people protested against apartheid for months in massive demonstrations but it did not bring legislation to change the situation. When it became annoying and the rest of the world was alarmed, the Government simply abolished the organizations that were behind the protest, passed the Suppression of Communism Act and Terrorism Act which effectively declared all peaceful protest to be illegal, made peaceful protesters into criminals and traitors, and apartheid continued. Liberation will never come by asking the Government to change, for the System will only yield under extreme pressure . . . and tokenists are scared of being involved in any pressure situation. So they talk tokenism, and vote Progressive, and hope the 'Nats' get in.

Tokenists sense the dynamics of the kingdom thrusting up from below but they blunt them into reforms that will simply produce a reformed civil religion, an improved model of the *status quo* society. Tokenism has not a sniff of salvation nor even the distant sound of liberation and tries to see by candlelight even when the sun is coming up.

Christian activists are the fourth group to be distinguished amongst Christian believers, those who recognize that there is a need of fundamental change in the conceptualization, construction and activity of both church and society, and devote themselves to discovering and working towards those alternatives.

The Christian Institute fell into this group. It was not a church denomination but an independent collection of Christians who were not weighed down with the necessity of dragging the cumbersome weight of a national ecclesiastical structure behind them like a reluctant elephant going in reverse. People of all races and shades of belief joined it in a free association which was in a constant state of change and development itself, producing many headaches and tensions, because it was doing something. Its quest for a Christian answer led it constantly closer to involvement with those who actually suffered under oppression and were victimized by the system, and struggled against it. This quest for a living faith in the fundamentals of a living society led the Christian Institute into action and reflection upon that action and further action, and because of this it came under great strain within its own membership situation, with its projects in the community, and from the Government.

It was there that I learnt that the true role of love is not to avoid the struggle but to empower it, for there were times of tension in the Christian Institute when we were so stretched that the bonds of caring and service were the only things that held us together. Flashes of eternity caught in the odd moments of time, precious parcels of words or looks or touch given from one to another, still fill my memories of those years which cannot yet be written down – for ultimately love is the only thing that holds Christian activists together. That is their liberation.

Such Christian activists recognize what it took me so many frustrated years to realize, that ecclesiastical organizations of the churches are not the instruments of liberation into God's kingdom, but the religious parts of society needing to be liberated. Such groups operate within the church body and within many other parts of society, and it is in such groups that people experience the ecumenity of the kingdom.

The idea that church leaders in high level discussions will liberate us from our denominational divisiveness is incredibly naïve. When Christians are sufficiently concerned to liberate themselves by acting the Jesus way in society, they will experience that ecumenical unity, and then the bishops and conferences can stitch it into a Constitution if they want to. Acts 2, when the Holy Spirit was poured out on the apostles and empowered them to go into the world to make disciples for the kingdom, comes before Acts 15, when the Council of Jerusalem came together to authorize it. It must always be that way.

The Christian activist groups in and between and outside the churches in South Africa today are crucial elements in the liberation struggle both in transforming the churches, and in teasing out the specific Christian contribution to liberation. For a very obvious reason I do not want to mention any names. The Christian Institute activated the scene for sixteen years, and was then clobbered out of existence on the early morning of 19 October 1977 as effectively as any other activist group in history. The CI, for all its faults, was for liberation, which is why the system decreed it had to go. They should have remembered the story of the resurrection: there are far more groups of Christians like that today.

The fifth classification for Christians in the struggle is when they forget any self-conscious attempt to justify themselves as Christians and become *simply liberated people* in God's world, as Jesus was. There is no evidence that he wanted to be anything else. Christians do not have a special sort of suffering when they are oppressed, or a special sort of anguish when they are in prison: they are just people. They are simply human beings struggling for emancipation from the oppression and restrictions which inhibit their full liberated life as God's children. They do not love any more than others, or suffer any more than others, or die any better than others, or have a grasp of wisdom or courage which is excluded from others: what they have is a faith which puts all this together in a way of life. They become aware that the liberation movement is itself a sign and a response to the kingdom, the jurisdiction of God in the affairs of men. Their concept of God and his purposes is no longer limited to a vested interest in its religious expression. There is an incredible relief, a deep satisfaction and encouragement, when all the fuss and palaver is stripped away from God and you can relate to him as they did to Jesus, in the ordinary affairs of life.

The difference between liberated Christians and other people is the faith which enables them to understand what is happening and what they are doing in the wider and deeper dimensions. They are living in the liberated world as God sees it.

For many Christian people reality has been frightened out of existence and they live in a world of make-believe. Those who have gone through the hocus-pocus and come out on the other side to live in the real world of people – instead of the extremely limited world of the bourgeosie – come to discover the bubbling joy and power of the Christian faith. They are usually much too busy to theologize about it.

Centuries of indoctrination over the holy nature of the church have induced in many of us a sort of blindness to our role in the world, a subservience to a mystique which owes everything to superstition and nothing at all to Jesus of Nazareth. Not everything that calls itself his Body has an equal claim to being filled with his Spirit. It was not so in the time of the New Testament, it is not been so throughout history, and it is not so today.

Many of our difficulties about the role of the church are clarified when we analyse its different aspects as follows: *the World Church*, focussed in world-wide Councils of Churches, or Conferences of a single denomination; *the National Church,* which may be denominations or councils of churches within a particular country; *the Local Church*, which is the local congregation of any one of hundreds of different denominations; and *the Ecclesia Group* which is a small gathering of Christian disciples operating in any of the above, or outside them in any other place in the world.

The Western Church organizations and institutions at global, national, or local level have a crucial role to play but they are themselves inextricably mixed up with the capitalist militarist nationalist world and it is vital that we should assess the effect of this upon them. They are highly organized religious businesses, dominated by the expertise of financiers and administrators and the primacy of nurturing their investment funds, designed on hierarchical lines, employing a careful selection process for the elimination of radical elements in the emergence of leadership material, shielding their leaders from the rank and file, susceptible to the manipulation and corruption of ecclesiastical power which is so absolute, weighed down with premises, subject to the wily operation of a system of emotional and procedural traditions which out-manoeuvre any converting agency, and not infrequently diverts protest into spurious sentiment.

These church institutions include many individualist power seekers of all colours who enslave people instead of freeing them, inhibited by pious and expensive administrations, debilitating protocol and irrelevant precedents, devoted to the preservation of themselves as institutions, massive expressions of Western trans-national ideology. Many churchmen present an elitist bourgeois image through their life-style, attitudes and associates which sets them apart from the oppressed people and their quest for a new life.

Such operations need liberating. They are not acceptable to those who seek a country or a world with shared leadership, corporate community development, and a banishment of affluence and poverty. The path to liberation is trodden by the ecclesia groups which operate within and outside the larger church institutions.

In South Africa there are such small groups of Christians who are involved in the struggle for liberation and able to reflect on this experience. These groups do not have conferences about ecumenicity: they experience it. They do not argue about violence: they suffer it. The question of whether the church should be involved in politics does not trouble them: politicians and policemen are hounding them into jail for following Christ. They are not afraid of most Marxists because you know where you are with them: they are not comfortable with many church-men because you don't know where you are with them.

They don't become involved in endless arguments about piety versus the social gospel. The only holiness they know arises in the context of the liberation struggle. The fruits of the Spirit are not emotional ecstasies but the nitty-gritty of life, the cir-cumstances of society in which love emerges through hatred, joy through misery, peace through torment, patience through ten-sion, kindness through cruelty, loyalty through duplicity, humility through arrogance, and selflessness through rampant self-centredness.

All the church has a task to accomplish but the key to the involvement of Christ in the struggle for liberation is in the ecclesia groups, the free-ranging bands of disciples who may make many mistakes, may sometimes be brushed aside, but constantly forge ahead in ways which the more institutionalized church is unable to follow at such a stage.

When the early settlers were seeking to find a way into the interior of Africa there were no roads at all. It was impossible to take wagons and herds of cattle down game paths, or through single file tracks trodden by the indigenous people, or to scale mountain ranges except by exhausting adventures to find a suitable passage, or cross a river without finding a shallow place to ford. Small bands of voorlopers were sent out ahead, some-times days or weeks ahead, to forge a way into the unknown for the main body to follow in due course and establish in the spirit of settlement what had been won through the spirit of adventure.

The church should not be afraid of its voorlopers: it needs them. It should support the ecclesia groups and enable them to go on ahead and make a highway through the unknown lest the church body remain for ever lost in the desolate places, unable to find its way through the difficult terrain, a Body lost, bogged down and dug in, which needs the breath of a new spirit to enable it to stand upon its feet. The ecclesia groups may sometimes make mistakes, but it is only the ecclesia groups that can show us the way to go.

9

From Traditional Theology
to Contextual Theology

Situation 1. During the Black Consciousness era one of my colleagues was Oshadi Phakathi ('Nurse Jane') who was involved with a group of young black students in Mamelodi township near Pretoria. They were putting themselves through a research course in liberation and were persuaded somewhat reluctantly to have a weekend retreat on Liberation and Christianity. When Oshadi mentioned that the course would be led by a white man and that they would be staying in his home, there was nearly a revolution on the spot. In such circumstances it was quite impossible for me to start with a traditional exposition of Moses the Liberator, or Jesus the Liberator, or the incarnation, or the kingdom of God. The only starting point was their own experience of involvement in the liberation struggle.

Situation 2. During my detention, when it appeared that the initial period of intensive interrogation was over and I was to be kept in solitary confinement for some time, I knew I must do something to keep myself occupied and because I yearned for the children decided to write to them about the Christian faith – in my head. It was Christmas 1981, walking round and round in the tiny exercise yard at the police cells in Brixton, Johannesburg. I had taught some of the children in a 'Confirmation' class years before but I knew that no traditional approach to Christianity would grip them now. I asked myself: What are they most concerned about? What affects all young people? Girls and boys, things, problems, and the struggle to feel at home and wanted in a world that seemed so aggressive. During the next few weeks I wrote 237 paragraphs about God in the context of present day experience and inscribed it on toilet paper. Later I took a chance to smuggle it out with another prisoner which failed, for it never arrived. All I have left are the titles of the paragraph headings, written on the blank pages between the Testaments in my Bible: 'Who do men say that I am? – the human experience of God. In the context of Sex, Possessions, Pollution, a World View, and the Sense of Lostness.'

Situation 3. Later, I spent eleven months as an ordinary awaiting trial prisoner in the historical monument of Johannesburg's Fort. About one hundred other whites, who the authorities would not release on bail, were there for every crime including murder, robbery with violence, theft, vagrancy, fraud, bilking, and drug running. The cells were wire cages seven feet high and when I lay on my back with outstretched arms I touched all four walls at the same time. Each cell had a rusty galvanized shit pot, a bed mat, and some filthy blankets. In the yard were three toilets none of which had seats, with walls three foot high but no doors, and several rows of basins all in the open air: the most public lavatory I had ever seen. In the corner of the yard stood a door before which we queued for 'graze up'. In the exercise period some tried to play games if a ball was available, and others to walk up and down, but there were so many people that the dodging and bumping made it difficult. Many just sat and talked, or just sat. Sometimes there were fights, or public sexual performances, or bullying, or arguments, or grief, or comments on those who were high on smuggled drugs. To one side stood the open door to the Visitors Room where twenty people were crammed together and had to shout through the bars to be heard in a bedlam of sound.

In this environment I was asked to take morning prayers. Clearly, it would have been utterly useless to rehash a normal church service or a typical church prayer in either language or subject matter. It had to arise directly out of our own experience there and then, the experience of prisoners with other prisoners in a prison yard – and it is incredible how much of the Bible was written by or about people in prisons. From that time onwards I seldom had a free moment in the yard because so many wanted to talk something through.

The point is simply this: our theology must arise out of the context of our lives. There is a place for studying the traditional doctrines of the church which have been handed down from generation to generation but they should be kept in that place, for theology must be contextual if it is to be a channel for an experience of the liberating power of God. All the doctrines we have inherited were contextual when they first arose but they must be reminted in the coinage of today.

One of my former colleagues in the Institute of Contextual Theology in Johannesburg has written:

> I do not believe in a congregation that leaves its problems at home to come and worship on Sunday morning. It was my contention in Kagiso where I was ministering that the congregation should not give me a wrong picture of what they are. Whereas during the week they live in their 'overalls', on Sunday they buy special clothes which they cannot even afford, to come and pretend to me that they have no problems. I feel that the congregation must come with their problems on Sunday so that those problems form the context of the 'sermon'. The problems must disturb our formal irrelevant services into services that serve the people, services which brainstorm their problems and thus theologise (act). That is what I understand by the contextualisation of theology (Frank Chikane).

The understanding of Christianity which has inspired and integrated me has not come from the books or from the Bible in which I subsequently checked it out, but in my overalls thinking about what was going on in and behind every day. In these pages I have set out some of the context which is part of the life in which I have been doing theology: the God who is in the us-moments; the structures of society; the conflict of race and class; the elite and the grass roots; revolution; struggle; and the torment within the church which is spearheaded by the activity of the ecclesia groups. This is the context of my life in which any understanding of God must arise. I am so conscious of my own shortcomings, shallowness and blindness that I find it most difficult to write this chapter which will inevitably be inadequate. But I must seek to summarize some of the insights which seem to be relevant for anyone who would lift up their head and go out to seek the stature of a whole liberated integrated person in this world, which is what the disciples of the kingdom are all about.

In the context of life's experience in Southern Africa we become aware of certain dynamics which are working within this human society, like yeast in flour. As gravity works on every physical molecule, as life depends on continuing breath, so does human society find its resource in categories of living which lie within its nature and give cogency and direction to the understanding and fulfilment of our corporate life.

There is a *spiritual dynamic*. In this world, in which we have been taught that everything that matters can be measured, or bought, or controlled through power politics, there is an extra-human dimension to our living which is beyond our human power to control but into which we can enter. Although the world appears to be ruled by the principalities and powers (the financial, militarist or political rulers of the world) these cannot overcome the true ultimates, the extra-human factors which are present amongst us and against which might shall not prevail.

I call that dimension God, and believe he was most completely in Jesus of Nazareth, and I worship him. But I do not wish to argue about this with people who call the extra-human dimension Yahweh, or Allah, or the Buddha, or Dialectical Materialism, or the Rules by which human society operates, or whatever. What I contend for is a recognition of the existence and obedience to this extra-human dimension. The experience of the dynamic is available to us all, and I have known it with all types of people. Our task is to witness to the dynamic not to argue over its name. If others recognize in me that I have 'been with Jesus' (Acts 4.13) and if as a result of this they 'want to see Jesus' (John 12.21) that is well and good. The spiritual dynamic is about 'the Way, the Truth and the Life', which comes from the depth of our being.

Life is full of god-forsaken moments when it seems that all is finished, that death rules, when tragedy is unrelieved, when there is nothing left to hope for. Yet it is in these moments that the spiritual extra-human dynamics arise and bubble over. In the god-forsaken times of life God becomes known. In such experiences we become aware of the on-going purpose that will not be defeated within us, and it is this that sends the shafts of joy and courage, assurance and love running through the people who have heard it. Faith only grows when it is tested in the struggle. It appears to be very difficult for oppressors or people in the affluent end of society to hear this note. But the oppressed hear it: freedom is in the air.

We are spiritual creatures, made in the image of God; and responding to that dynamic within ourselves is the source of liberation. Jesus says: 'Come! Stretch out your hand! Get up on your feet! Be!'

There is an *ecological dynamic*. We live in one integrated world in which all things have a common relationship and are inter-related. When Christians say that God was in Christ reconciling the world to himself they mean that God does not differentiate between the spiritual and the secular world but has brought them together, and that whilst politics and economics and religion have different functions they all operate in the same sphere, and are mutually dependent and responsible to one another. All things are sacraments of God's presence and the making of right material decisions to make good wholesome use of the earth is an essential part of our spiritual life. The wholeness of truth liberates.

The incarnation is a truly ecological event and when Jesus says that he brought the truth to make us free he is saying that as we respond to the jurisdiction of God in all the affairs of this world, including the material, we shall find the freedom which is the fullness of life.

The most polluted part of this planet is humanity, and our battle to preserve the world from spoilation begins with the battle to convert humankind to wholeness. Some oppressors have raped the earth of its goodness and other oppressors have sought to rape us of our godliness too by making us constantly grovel in our sinfulness, and never stir beyond the mud of our degradation and dependency. To this the Lord God Almighty says: 'Piffle! You are made in my image, I find you good, you have the power to become my children: Be!'

There is a dynamic stirring within us, and as we take of

the things of the earth and make them whole, so do we bring healing to ourselves. When Christians need a focus for their faith they do not take flowers from the field, or stories of their ancestors, or images of gods or magic tablets or stones. They take bread and wine which they have made themselves, constructed out of their own ecology, and through these they focus on the eternal realities.

There is a *cultural dynamic*. Our communal humanity is not a strange far-off proposition that we may succeed in growing into one day, but an actual realized experience, something that happens when we come together in quest of liberated communities. The answer to disunity is something we actually experience in ecumenicity, not when we talk about it but when we practise it. The emphasis is not upon false fumbling after expressions of our failure, but in the enjoyment of our acceptance of one another and our awareness of a new community about us and within us. People in the struggle share their cultures; they do not fight to destroy one another but to build one another up, and experience the foretaste of the new society.

How many times have I sat in my study, or in someone's garden, with people of all races and backgrounds in a shared quest for liberation, and known the dynamics of community wrapping us about. For all our different ways of being human – we love! Why call it anything else! This mutuality knits our differences into a simple rich tapestry of living togetherness. When people live and work together in quest of the Way, they experience community, and know their unity. The Bible is on the side of the prophets, the freedom fighters, the prisoners, detainees and exiles and the oppressed, through whose leadership the new community comes into being.

There is an *economic dynamic*. Those of us who live in Southern Africa are not excluded from the concerns of the rest of the world, we know, but we are not bound by the understanding and decisions of the northern parts either. We do not accept the concept of a world in the terms of a US versus USSR struggle which is foisted upon us.

We know that the view of the world set out in the West is false. It may seem a blessing to the West, but capitalism is a

curse to all the world. We know the Western propaganda ploy
that sees itself as the servant of God against the evils of the
Communist East is false. Beset with enormous problems we look
within ourselves to find the seeds of a new socialist economy
that is rooted in the poor and oppressed. The priorities of Jesus
in his relationships with the poor and the rich, his teaching on
sufficiency, his concept of sharing, are not pious platitudes but
hard factual principles for this dynamic of economic life which
we have to take in hand and work out. The little ones shall
lead us, it will be a people-based economy and the dynamic that
rises within us does not see life in the service of economic growth,
but demands that economics is there to promote living.

There is a *political dynamic*. Democracy it must be, but it is
clear to us that neither Westminster nor Washington has solved
the problem of devising a government by the people, and we
rejected their solutions years ago. What new systems will be
devised we cannot know until we are free to discuss them and
experiment, but in our present experience our models are
participatory at every level. We are well aware that democrat-
ization is not neat and power-centred, that it is wide-ranging
and untidy and constantly breaking out to new forms of life,
like the Holy Spirit; that it is not stinting of its energies like the
profit makers, but deals in profusions and abundance and
wastefulness and enjoyment like the seeds in our lands and our
loins, or unproductive laughter and unnecessary love. The
dynamic prompting a new democracy is in a constant state
of growth and development and new experience, a politics subservient to life.

And it is a struggle. An experience of the norm of life is not
a sheltered one, a heaven, but a struggle of good against evil in
which we find the fullness of life, and that is the life of which
the Bible speaks. The Bible does not expect the rulers of this
world to give up easily, to heed reasonable requests, to move
quietly in the correct direction. The quest for godly government
on earth, for obedience to the dynamics of political peace and
prosperity is a struggle of good overcoming evil as we read the
scriptures. Strife is not an aberration, conflict is not out of
the ordinary, the struggle for perfection is a condition of life
until the kingdom comes, a toil from which from time to time

we must 'come apart and rest a while'. The dynamic which rises within us is the awareness of our privilege to be steady, clear-eyed and level-headed (some of the time) in this struggle to defeat the evil and enable the good which is inherent in everything around us, to come out into harvest.

Winding strongly above the cacophony of the struggle in the South of Africa comes the clear mellifluous call of the herald's trumpet announcing the dawning of the freedom for which we strive. It peals from the gaunt grey ranges speckled with red hot pokers; it bowls across the dusty green of the bushveld and the rustling mealielands; it bounds from koppie to koppie over the wide plains of the Highveld; it rushes along the white sands of the beaches swept by the surge and cymbal crash of the breakers; through the desolate Dumping Grounds, the lonely farms, through the crowded life of the matchbox townships, through the white suburbs overweight with their affluence, the people lift their heads to the notes which promise liberation and life.

People may use a different notation to write them down. Some catch only the simple air and others experiment with accompaniments; some use the tonic sol-fa of Marxism; others the stringy harmonies of the East, some find the herald's trumpet sets their feet to stomping out the rhythms in the drumming of daily life, yet others compose broad symphonies around it. Even the tone deaf feel the vibrations.

Whatever their instrument or their score, they are responding to the same pealing proclamation of hope and purpose for a new life which rises up within their being, and urges them on.

For Christians who have ears to hear it is the certain sound of the kingdom of God amongst us in the now.

We are God's children now, heirs of Christ, the Jesus people, those called to be saints together. We can accept the reality of forgiveness and new life, and put away the emphasis upon our sinfulness and inadequacy which is unscriptural and untrue, and walk away from the dependency which leads us to accept that we are incapable of taking new initiatives, or clinging to our sinfulness as an excuse for going no further. Be liberated from that burden and start being a citizen of the real kingdom.

Stand on your feet in the new life that works and exults in letting the movement of the kingdom come through. Accept the responsibility and the wonder of being a co-worker with God in the great enterprise of his way on planet earth.

The sound of freedom stirs assurance and encouragement into our consciousness because we do not have to be afraid (Matt. 10.26) and we are promised the victory (Luke 21.19). Once we have taken the measure of the struggle that lies ahead, and breathed deep into our lungs the spirit of the liberated life together, there is in our deepest being peace and joy and hope.

10

Into the Fire

My trial for High Treason began in the Supreme Court in Pretoria on 7 February 1983. Early in the morning they took me from the prison to a large windowless dungeon below the court and for an hour I paced around reading the graffiti with which generations of prisoners had decorated every inch of wall space. There was none of the usual smutty sex: it was a political commentary on all the major trials for the previous twenty years with names, dates and sentences, comments, two complete versions of the Freedom Charter which some had known by heart, and many Psalms and encouraging messages.

Up above, in the pseudo-classical Main Court I was deeply moved, first at the solid phalanx of my family who looked so good with their suits and dresses and button-holes, cushions and thermos flasks and sandwiches; they reminded me of visitors to the State President's garden party who had ended up at the Wanderer's cricket field by mistake; secondly, by the support from friends, churchfolk, diplomats and visitors from near and far; and thirdly, by an unaccustomed sense of humility and honour because the bench in which I sat was first used by Nelson Mandela and our comrades in the Rivonia Trial twenty years before. Twenty years: don't think it.

The prosecution were out to prove that I had acted for many years as a member of the banned African National Congress, and were putting in my Statement to the Security Police, and other evidence. The defence was that my actions had arisen directly from my Christian commitment, and that the statement had been made under duress. The defence team, Kathy Satchwell and Lionel Bowman, headed by Ernie Wentzel at his confident best, took on the thirteen Security Police witnesses one by one. Called to give evidence at this 'trial within a trial' I spoke in public for the first time in six years, a quarter of which had been in prison. After two weeks Mr Justice P. J. Van der Walt announced his decision that the statement was *not* acceptable as evidence for reasons he would give later in the trial, and asked the Prosecutor to proceed. The Prosecutor requested an adjournment. After lunch, in a few dramatic moments that none of us will ever forget, the case was postponed for two months, the Attorney General withdrew the certificate precluding bail, and I was released for two months and a thousand Rand.

I had not the slightest intention of leaving the country and looked forward to making a Christian contribution to the struggle when the court reassembled, but a few days before the resumption I received information which totally altered the situation. It became clear that the Security Police, not the Attorney General were the controlling influence and they did not propose to let me go, whatever happened. Subpoena were reissued to several of my friends to give evidence against me, which meant they would go to jail for refusing. It was clear that legal prudence would set limitations upon the political advantages to be gained from the trial which was my major object in going on with it. Under these circumstances, commitment demanded that I leave to continue the struggle from outside the country, and once this was clear I did not hesitate, but it was the most hurtful decision I have ever made in my life. Our comrades in prison continue their witness: their presence in prison is a potent political fact, a constant witness to liberty that challenges all the world. I knew they would insist that I should be free to fight for freedom if I could. My body was stripped by the Security Police; my mind was stripped in fighting for life in the interrogation and the trial; but leaving the country stripped my soul. I do not know if the wound will ever heal, and do not want to write about it any more. I would have been quite happy to have been caught.

Stupid people have pressed me to recount the details of how I left the country which is clearly impossible so I have made up several stories to satisfy the most persistent. The one I prefer is a sequel to the magnificent lies told by Donald Woods when he left, explaining how he had swum the crocodile infested Caledon river to reach Lesotho. It was much easier for me because of the drought – I walked across on the crocodiles' backs.

Seriously, I got a lift to near the border and walked the rest through forests and mealie-lands and down rocky kranzes to the willows, with the glorious Mother Sun of Africa rising before me. Even as I reached the river and wondered where to cross I saw a line of naked foot-prints through the mud going down into the water and emerging on the other side and followed them without a pause. The water was cold but it only came to my knees. Why did the story of Jesus and John the Baptist flash into my mind as I waded through, thrusting out little waves, and walked up the bank into the new life that lay ahead?

Very soon after my arrival in London I attended a Press Conference at which I stated my intention to continue the struggle against apartheid in the West. The main ingredients of that struggle are two-fold.

First, it is to weaken and pull up the roots of apartheid in Western civilization, ensuring that those who support the apartheid system by dealing with it in any way are made to feel the unacceptability of their contemptuous role in any decent company on earth. This applies to politicians, to bankers, to investors, sports people, entertainers, academics, tourists and purchasers of South African goods in the local supermarkets. Apartheid exists because of the support it receives from Western civilization and everything that people have read or seen about the appalling cruelty and injustice of the apartheid regime is sustained by the roots of that system in the civilization of the Western world. People must be made to realize that this is a matter of shame, and for Christians, an evil act in support of heresy, and that the association should be ended forthwith.

The other aspect of the struggle for people in the West is to align themselves with the liberators, whether these are struggling in different ways inside South Africa, or in exile. The West cannot liberate South Africa, the oppressed people are their own liberators, but there are many ways in which their struggle to humanize society by liberating it from crippling oppression can be aided and assisted from outside.

What I had failed to realize, and I have discovered since that it is the common experience of many people from the Third World who come to Europe or North America, is that the norms of Western civilization are the norms of the oppressive society which you have fought so long and now left behind.

I do not feel it is my place to tell the West or the North what they should do about their own society at this stage, but it may be interesting to recount how the West appears to exiles, and it is certainly my duty to set out ways in which the South African experience may suggest ways in which Western people can evaluate themselves.

Apartheid is not a different type of civilization from the West but is the hard refined cutting edge of it. Apartheid is not a blot on Western civilization but the heart of it. Apartheid is the eye-piece through which you can see the whole, a microcosm, a revelation of what Western civilization is really all about.

At some of the workshops I have attended since coming into exile, groups have sought to analyse the question: 'How can sincere Christian people like white South Africans produce this evil apartheid society?' As people probe the attitudes of South African Christian society . . . it suddenly dawns upon them that they are describing their own. South Africa is honest about it and puts it into its laws, but the practice of colour prejudice, economic exploitation, spiritual blindness and hypocrisy, on a major scale, are the common experience of millions of people in the world which is dominated and administered by the West.

The battle that we fight against oppression in apartheid South Africa is our own version of a battle that is being fought against oppression in the principalities and powers of all the world.

Apartheid is said to be a heresy which must be destroyed (rather than a sin which can be forgiven) because it takes fractions of the truth and distorts them, making an evil of them, and does it in the name of God. Throughout history it has been the task of Christians to root out heresy and expunge it and it is still part of the task today.

Emperor worship, in which the Caesar was elevated to the status of god and worshipped above all other things, is by no means dead in these days. The promotion of nationalist and patriotic ideals, the advocacy of so-called Western Christian civilization, and its parallel in the unquestioned oblation paid to the fear of Communism, is of the same twisted morality as the Jews who cried: 'We have no God but Caesar' and claimed to do so in the name of the living God.

The West worships Mammon. The pursuit of profit, the encouragement of unemployment in order to promote further profit, the growth of a 'free' economy in the West which means the freedom to use your muscle to exploit others, and the use of the whole Third World in the same way that the South African Government uses its Homelands as dumping grounds, is unjust on the face of it, and heretical when people imply that it is part of the Christian way of life.

There is a blindness in the West which horrifies those who have come out of the darkness to see a great light in their own land, and use that light to interpret the world around them. People in the West do not know that they are oppressors or part of an oppressive society: they think that they are Liberals and Reformers and do not recognize that these are the garments worn by oppressors. It is incredible that people do not suspect the forms of democracy in the West which enable governments which are approved by a minority of the population to have total power for years at a time and no one does a thing about it. The claims to have a free press and television service should not blind us to the fact that an occasional excursion into genuine criticism does not prevent the whole of the media from being dominated by an elite whose ideology is oppressive, paternalist, un-Christian, and in frightening similarity to the subtle steering of opinion in a totalitarian country.

It soon became apparent to me that the level of effectiveness of Western commitment to change in South Africa could only be raised if people in the West became concerned for their own liberation. If you are to help us to be able to be ourselves we must help you to be able to be yourselves. If we are all involved in the same struggle it is those of us who have been involved for longer and thus have more experience, those of us who are involved at a more critical stage, that are likely to have some awareness to be shared. Many Western people seem to live within the parameters imposed upon them by the principalities and powers of Western civilization, and are sunk into an apathetic acceptance of the *status quo* in state and church, unable to see that they need liberating themselves, and quite unaffected by the fervour and enthusiasm of those who know what the struggle is about.

A liberating movement from blindness and oppression is taking place throughout Western civilization which is as fundamental and far-reaching as any in history, including the Early Christian era and the Reformation. This surging movement is easier to see in lands like South Africa where oppression is more stark and the spirit of liberation is more advanced. We are in the middle of a revolution.

This stirring, itching, yearning for fundamental change is neither wrong nor juvenile nor leftist, but the correct heart of Christianity, the genuine Jesus thing, the point of it all. We must not allow ourselves to be put off, pushed off, or bought off by those who counsel gradual gentlemanly improvements. The kingly rule of God on earth which we are born again to see means a revolution in terms of politics, economics, culture, ecology and faith, and people must be liberated from their enslavement to the stereotypes, prejudices and powers of contemporary life through becoming involved in the struggle for the kingdom. It is here, and it is now.

The church institutions are not the source or instruments of salvation but the religious parts of society to be liberated. They are not an army but a battlefield. They are spheres in which we may carry on the struggle within society, and this often begins with an awareness of the judgment that is upon us. The churches are religious dependents of the capitalist, nationalistic systems of the West and identify themselves with the heresies of civil religions on numerous occasions. Modern religious bodies can be as misguided and irrelevant to the purposes of God as were the Scribes and Pharisees.

The prevailing thought that the churches can be changed by

their leadership is not derived from scripture, nor checked out in history, but from the categories of Western power elite structures. Church unity does not come from the top down but from the bottom up. Christian influence is not spread by building strong magnificent towers of Babel, whether of organization or bricks and mortar, but by taking flickering tongues of flame to the ends of the earth. God does not institute himself in temples of stone or legislation, but in a mobile tent constantly moved and recreated in the presence of the people's other activities (Acts 7.44–51). Church renewal does not come from building schemes or colleges or conferences but from groups of renewed people. People are not renewed by imparting emotions or ideas to them but by the release of life and love amongst them – which means that churches are not usually changed by traditional 'church people' but by 'outsiders' who come with something new.

Christians believe that they have a message to give the world which is of supreme importance, but our theology is something which 'the masses' and many of our own congregations find supremely irrelevant. If we approach this by endeavouring to adapt inherited traditional dogmatism to contemporary circumstances, or by seeking to calculate what is the minimum of the past that is essential for our people to accept, then we are lost before we start. It is like giving a bridegroom a book entitled 'The Guide to Happy Marriage' without a bride.

We have to get into the actual experiences from everyday life (as Jesus and Paul and Luther and Wesley did in their day) and let the theology arise out of reflection on the living, as they did. Scripture and history are not the instigators of belief but the corroborators. Our theology must be rooted in our own experience.

After the Second World War there was an explosion of theological reflection which was the breath of life to many of us at that time and I well remember taking down the *Letters and Papers from Prison* in a Durban bookshop, and feeling that Dietrich Bonhoeffer had written it directly to me. But in the years that followed the theology vaporized into unreachable academic clouds which evaporated above the deserts left by the controversies over the Death of God. Then to our arid

Western minds came the torrential downpour of Liberation Theology from Latin America, Blacks and Women, where people were struggling for the fullness of abundant life in their own environment. Western Christians fell on this like prospectors on a gold strike but it was all second hand. It was not grounded in their own liberation struggle for they were working a claim that belonged to someone else.

The rediscovery of a living faith in the West depends upon the involvement of Christians in the liberation struggle of the masses in the West: and because churches are mostly structured to nurture the colleges, conferences and congregations in aloofness from the actual concerns of the masses, the churches require considerable recasting themselves before they can hope to take part in a religious revival, that is, be liberated.

Liberation faith demands that some of us should admit and confront our concern about the concept of God. We need not regret the passing of a Sky-God who never was; nor bother because the stars are held in their courses by gravity instead of his fingers. We can boldly assert that nations are not blessed by their adherence to this or that religion, but by their obedience to the laws of the kingdom built into human society which are a-religious. We need not grieve because Christian preoccupation with life after death has been replaced by preoccupation with life; nor that the self-centred introspective concern for the inner life of holiness has been left behind in an others-centred quest for sanctification which experiences the fruit of the Spirit in the contextual circumstances of modern daily life.

Sometimes our nostalgic hankerings after reflections or echoes of the past leave us stumbling in the fog of un-being-ness, which Jesus undoubtedly went through himself. We need to hear the voice which pierced the bandaged senses of Lazarus: 'Loose him and let him go.'

Our task is not to plug this or that idea of God, but to be people who incarnate God. What grabs people is not how you grasp the concept of Father or Mother, Son or Spirit, but how the Divine comes through you in your loving. God is not a set of precepts, nor an ecclesiastical ordination nor a baptism nor a piece of bread and wine, nor an argument: God is love.

It is quite improper for us to insist that others accept our beliefs, as a pre-condition for our involvement in the liberation struggle: those who make such demands are oppressors par excellence. Our task is to become involved in the struggle, where we are, for justice, or peace, or fulfilment, as normal human beings, and if there is anything distinctive about our Christian belief it is for other people to recognize it and ask about it if they will. They will.

Our constituency is not the middle-class churchy intellectual, for though there is a ministry within such groups these are not the spring of liberation, and salvation is not from them. It comes through the so-called lower-class, unchurched, un-intellectual 'masses'. Our task is not to go to them and tell them how to be saved, but to live with them and love with them and learn from them in what salvation and liberation consists. When we stop being 'them' and 'us' we start being liberated.

I spent many years in South Africa trying to help the 'poor blacks' into a better life before discovering that I was the one who needed help. Western peoples, bemused by generations of self-deception about their liberal attitudes and love of freedom, are still a long way behind the Third World in the quest for liberation. The masses in the West do not have as clear an idea of oppression or of liberation as do the masses elsewhere but it is from them that the answer will come. It is the task of con-cerned Christians to hang in there, learning to be just people, just humans, just being and loving and enjoying and weeping and struggling and thinking and achieving – instead of moraliz-ing, reproving and admonishing.

We *may* go to our prayer meetings and services and theological study circles and spiritual exercises: but we *must* go to the pubs and clubs and Peace Movements and political activities and civic organizations and anti-apartheid groups and liberation movements, for without the latter the former are unreal. Those who are so busy running churches that they have no time for the normal life of the masses must realize that they may be religious but they are not following Jesus. Our task is not to make converts to Christianity but disciples for the kingdom.

I have dumped a lot of inherited concepts of God which were unhelpful, as I believe that Jesus did also. I have come into a renewed spiritual awareness out of the experiences through which I have passed. My problem now is not so much the nature of truth, not so much a willingness to obey truth, but the problem of fitting it all in and this is something that can only be achieved through community with others.

The key instrument for Liberation appears to be this community, the small ecclesia group at the local level, which may be within families, or churches, places of work, or neighbourhoods, or wherever small groups of disciples meet and seek to aid one another in liberation. They are people who live beyond the inherited ecclesiastical arrangements; who unite over denominational or racial or sexual barriers; who expect women or youths or blacks to lead them because they are emerging from oppression; who look to the wisdom of the poor and oppressed for their direction; and who recognize that love and understanding and service are the ends to which they must extend their skills and resources. We have to take very seriously the idea of rejecting the practice of organizing conferences to direct things from the top down, in favour of establishing small groups to explode things from the bottom up.

Such groups recognize that only a limited amount of their time can be spent on 'Church activities' for most of it should be spent in the wider world with 'publicans and sinners', or 'the common people', at dinner parties, in the market places and offices and workshops and homes where Jesus did his stuff. He did not turn the world upside down by attending Sanhedrin Committees or suiting his style to the Procurator's Banquets. Small groups of Christians – we the ecclesia – can be involved in the transforming life of the world when we discover for ourselves through local issues where we are oppressed, and experience liberation, and go for it.

I do not think it is a South African's task to spell out for anyone in the West where they need liberating, but I do know that it is from those experienced encounters in small groups that theology focussed on the masses will emerge, and the evangelical revival will erupt which will bring the liberation of Western civilization.

It is when people are dominated by the principalities and powers of this world that fear and pessimism and frustration bring them down, for it sometimes seems that the struggle will drag on forever, and that they will be unable to bring the revolution that the world so clearly needs. But whoever said we could? The very idea that we alone run the world, and are solely responsible for the revolution, is derived from the power-syndrome of the oppressors. To believe in the dawn on the darkest night is wonderful – but it does not mean that you can raise the Sun before her time.

Mere belief in the kingdom is not enough to enable it to happen overnight because the wonder of this transformation of society is something which has a time factor built into it. There is a Kairos time in history, a moment when events are ripe for development, times when there is the breaking in of new life to society which we can recognize but not control, anticipate but not manipulate, and on the brink of which we stand. Our task is to watch, to prepare, to make way for it by doing the essential catalytic task of offering faith.

Faith is a gift, which may come in a sudden blinding flash or as the result of a slow maturing process, and gives the Good News of a divine jurisdiction amongst us, the eruption of new hope and assurance that arises and transforms from the heart of the liberation movement. Faith is given in response to such proclamation, not to military or political or financial pressure. It is those of us who go out in the insecurity of faith who discover the power to bring down the mighty from their thrones, to give light to those who live in darkness and guide their feet into the way of peace.

Have you ever chopped down a tree? If you have you will know that it is a slow and constant process of driving the axe head into the heart of the wood, with chips flying everywhere, and no sign of success at all. The trunk stands straight and tall above you apparently as secure as it has been for years, and all your effort appears to be to no avail. There is not the slightest sign that you are succeeding. All you can do is to go on chopping. There can be no question of the tree gradually sliding over sideways, and when it gets half way, deciding to leave it there while you go away for lunch and come back later and carry on. It stands there vertical and apparently immovable despite all that you can do.

And then: the tree falls, and there is nothing that anyone can do to stop it. Its time has come. It is finished and it crashes to the ground. And all round it there is space for new life to grow. Amandla!

Other Orbis Books . . .

BLACK AND REFORMED
Apartheid, Liberation, and the Calvinist Tradition
by Allan Boesak
"In this collection, Allan Boesak continues to raise for those of us outside South Africa the issue of liberation of all people in that country. He creatively relates the black struggle for freedom in South Africa to the liberating message of Jesus Christ without sacrificing the universal note of the gospel." *James H. Cone, Union Theological Seminary, New York*

ISBN 0-88344-148-9 *192pp. Paper $8.95*

FAREWELL TO INNOCENCE
A Socio-Ethical Study on Black Theology and Black Power
by Allan Boesak
"Boesak provides a framework of review of current black consciousness, black power, black theology, and liberation theology and then offers a helpful, evolving black ethic. All the major black American and African theologians are included in summaries of these issues and are treated in adequate fashion. Boesak indicates his knowledge of the issues and in a brief concluding essay probes a black ethic that arises from oppressed peoples (e.g. black) and urges a reversal of much 20th century materialism 'to recapture what was sacred in the African community long before white people came—solidarity, respect for life, humanity, community.' " *Choice*

ISBN 0-88344-130-6 *197pp. Paper $8.95*

THE FINGER OF GOD
Sermons on Faith and Responsibility
by Allan Boesak
Foreword by Paul Lehmann
"Boesak is a South African student chaplain, and the excellent sermons collected here were written for his audience of young, liberated black Christians. Addressing hard political questions in a biblically centered fashion (scriptural passages introduce each sermon), Boesak more than meets his own criterion for good political preaching. Notes with background information on specific people and events will help American readers." *Library Journal*

ISBN 0-88344-135-7 *112pp. Paper $5.95*

SOUTH AFRICAN CHURCHES IN A REVOLUTIONARY SITUATION
by Marjorie Hope & James Young
"A useful historical outline, from the first settlement of the Dutch East
India Company in 1652, to the militant demonstrations by the Coloreds in
1980; a detailed *Who's Who* in the religious resistance to apartheid; brief
but often frank and revealing interviews with a broad spectrum of church
leaders and other activists. A modest but real contribution."

The Kirkus Reviews

ISBN 0-88344-466-6   *282pp. Paper $9.95*

THIRD WORLD RESOURCE DIRECTORY
A Guide to Organizations and Publications
edited by Thomas Fenton & Mary Heffron
A comprehensive guide which lists and describes hundreds of resources for
educators, committed church and political activists, and other concerned
citizens interested in Third World issues. Resources include organizations,
books, periodicals, pamphlets and articles, films, slide shows, videotapes,
and simulation games. Comprehensively cross-referenced and indexed.

"A highly valuable resource for educators, church activists, and all who
care about Third World people's needs for social justice. The directory
should be prominent in every reference library and in the office of every
social change agency."   *Bradford Chambers,*
Council on Interracial Books for Children

ISBN 0-88344-509-3   *304pp. Paper $17.95*

CHURCH VERSUS STATE IN SOUTH AFRICA
The Case of the Christian Institute
by Peter Walshe
Dr. Walshe, a South African scholar and author long resident in the U.S.,
traces the development of the South African Christian Institute. It came as
no surprise when the Institute, along with the remaining organizations of
the black consciousness movement, was banned in 1977, having made a
major contribution—and a lasting one—to the evolution of an indigenous
liberation theology. This book, based not only on the ample documentary
sources, but on personal interviews with all the leading participants, is
likely to remain a definitive account of a short but immensely influential
episode in modern South Africa's history.

ISBN 0-88344-097-0   *250pp. Cloth $19.95*